U.S. Department
of Transportation

**Federal Aviation
Administration**

Remote Pilot – Small
Unmanned Aircraft Systems
Study Guide

August 2016

Flight Standards Service
Washington, DC 20591

This page intentionally left blank.

Preface

The Federal Aviation Administration (FAA) has published the Remote Pilot – Small Unmanned Aircraft Systems (sUAS) Study Guide to communicate the knowledge areas you need to study to prepare to take the Remote Pilot Certificate with an sUAS rating airman knowledge test.

This Remote Pilot – Small Unmanned Aircraft Systems Study Guide is available for download from faa.gov. Please send comments regarding this document to afs630comments@faa.gov.

This page intentionally left blank.

Table of Contents

This page intentionally left blank.

Introduction

The information in this study guide was arranged according to the knowledge areas that are covered on the airman knowledge test for a Remote Pilot Certificate with a Small Unmanned Aircraft Systems Rating as required by Title 14 of the Code of Federal Regulations (14 CFR) part 107, section 107.73(a). The knowledge areas are as follows:

1. Applicable regulations relating to small unmanned aircraft system rating privileges, limitations, and flight operation;
2. Airspace classification, operating requirements, and flight restrictions affecting small unmanned aircraft operation;
3. Aviation weather sources and effects of weather on small unmanned aircraft performance;
4. Small unmanned aircraft loading;
5. Emergency procedures;
6. Crew resource management;
7. Radio communication procedures;
8. Determining the performance of small unmanned aircraft;
9. Physiological effects of drugs and alcohol;
10. Aeronautical decision-making and judgment;
11. Airport operations; and
12. Maintenance and preflight inspection procedures.

Obtaining Assistance from the Federal Aviation Administration (FAA)

Information can be obtained from the FAA by phone, Internet/e-mail, or mail. To talk to the FAA toll-free 24 hours a day, call 1-866-TELL-FAA (1-866-835-5322). To visit the FAA's website, go to www.faa.gov. Individuals can also e-mail an FAA representative at a local FSDO office by accessing the staff e-mail address available via the "Contact FAA" link at the bottom of the FAA home page. Letters can be sent to:

Federal Aviation Administration
800 Independence Ave, SW
Washington, DC 20591

FAA Reference Material

The FAA provides a variety of important reference material for the student, as well as the advanced civil aviation pilot. In addition to the regulations provided online by the FAA, several other publications are available to the user. Almost all reference material is available online at www.faa.gov in downloadable format. Commercial aviation publishers also provide published and online reference material to further aid the aviation pilot.

- Aeronautical Information Manual (AIM)
- Handbooks
- Advisory Circulars (ACs)
- Airman Certification Standards
- 14 CFR part 107

This page intentionally left blank.

Chapter 1:
Applicable Regulations

Be familiar with <u>14 CFR part 107</u> and all parts referenced in part 107, as well as <u>AC 107-2</u>.

See the ASA Reader Resource page to review the most current regulation and documents:
<u>www.asa2fly.com/reader/tpuas</u>

This page intentionally left blank.

Chapter 2:
Airspace Classification, Operating Requirements, and Flight Restrictions

Introduction

The two categories of airspace are: regulatory and nonregulatory. Within these two categories, there are four types: controlled, uncontrolled, special use, and other airspace. The categories and types of airspace are dictated by the complexity or density of aircraft movements, nature of the operations conducted within the airspace, the level of safety required, and national and public interest. *Figure 2-1* presents a profile view of the dimensions of various classes of airspace.

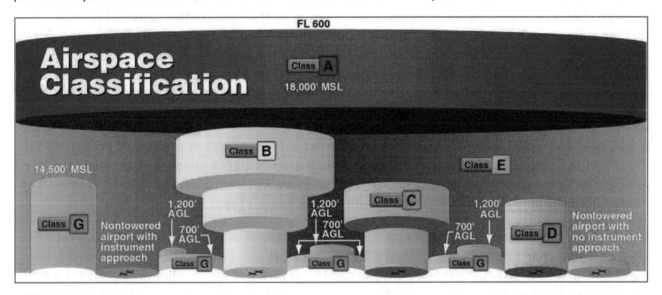

Figure 2-1. *Airspace profile.*

Controlled Airspace

Controlled airspace is a generic term that covers the different classifications of airspace and defined dimensions within which air traffic control (ATC) service is provided in accordance with the airspace classification. Controlled airspace that is of concern to the remote pilot is:

- Class B
- Class C
- Class D
- Class E

Class B Airspace

Class B airspace is generally airspace from the surface to 10,000 feet mean sea level (MSL) surrounding the nation's busiest airports in terms of airport operations or passenger enplanements. The configuration of each Class B airspace area is individually tailored, consists of a surface area and two or more layers (some Class B airspace areas resemble upside-down wedding cakes), and is designed to contain all published instrument procedures once an aircraft enters the airspace. A remote pilot must receive authorization from ATC before operating in the Class B airspace.

Class C Airspace

Class C airspace is generally airspace from the surface to 4,000 feet above the airport elevation (charted in MSL) surrounding those airports that have an operational control tower, are serviced by a radar approach control, and have a certain number of instrument flight rules (IFR) operations or passenger enplanements. Although the configuration of each Class C area is individually tailored, the airspace usually consists of a surface area with a five nautical mile (NM) radius, an outer circle with a ten NM radius that extends from 1,200 feet to 4,000 feet above the airport elevation. A remote pilot must receive authorization before operating in Class C airspace.

Class D Airspace

Class D airspace is generally airspace from the surface to 2,500 feet above the airport elevation (charted in MSL) surrounding those airports that have an operational control tower. The configuration of each Class D airspace area is individually tailored and, when instrument procedures are published, the airspace is normally designed to contain the procedures. Arrival extensions for instrument approach procedures (IAPs) may be Class D or Class E airspace. A remote pilot must receive ATC authorization before operating in Class D airspace.

Class E Airspace

Class E airspace is the controlled airspace not classified as Class A, B, C, or D airspace. A large amount of the airspace over the United States is designated as Class E airspace. This provides sufficient airspace for the safe control and separation of aircraft during IFR operations. Chapter 3 of the Aeronautical Information Manual (AIM) explains the various types of Class E airspace.

Sectional and other charts depict all locations of Class E airspace with bases below 14,500 feet MSL. In areas where charts do not depict a class E base, class E begins at 14,500 feet MSL. In most areas, the Class E airspace base is 1,200 feet above ground level (AGL). In many other areas, the Class E airspace base is either the surface or 700 feet AGL. Some Class E airspace begins at an MSL altitude depicted on the charts, instead of an AGL altitude. Class E airspace typically extends up to, but not including, 18,000 feet MSL (the lower limit of Class A airspace). All airspace above FL 600 is Class E airspace.

Federal Airways, which are shown as blue lines on a sectional chart, are usually found within Class E airspace. Federal Airways start at 1,200' AGL and go up to, but, not including 18,000' MSL.

In most cases, a remote pilot will not need ATC authorization to operate in Class E airspace.

Uncontrolled Airspace

Class G Airspace

Uncontrolled airspace or Class G airspace is the portion of the airspace that has not been designated as Class A, B, C, D, or E. It is therefore designated uncontrolled airspace. Class G airspace extends from the surface to the base of the overlying Class E airspace. A remote pilot will not need ATC authorization to operate in Class G airspace.

Special Use Airspace

Special use airspace or special area of operation (SAO) is the designation for airspace in which certain activities must be confined, or where limitations may be imposed on aircraft operations that are not part of those activities. Certain special use airspace areas can create limitations on the mixed use of airspace. The special use airspace depicted on instrument charts includes the area name or number, effective altitude, time and weather conditions of operation, the controlling agency, and the chart panel location. On National Aeronautical Charting Group (NACG) en route charts, this information is available on one of the end panels. Special use airspace usually consists of:

- Prohibited areas
- Restricted areas
- Warning areas
- Military operation areas (MOAs)
- Alert areas
- Controlled firing areas (CFAs)

Prohibited Areas

Prohibited areas contain airspace of defined dimensions within which the flight of aircraft is prohibited. Such areas are established for security or other reasons associated with the national welfare. These areas are published in the Federal Register and are depicted on aeronautical charts. The area is charted as a "P" followed by a number (e.g., P-40). Examples of prohibited areas include Camp David and the National Mall in Washington, D.C., where the White House and the Congressional buildings are located. [Figure 2-2]

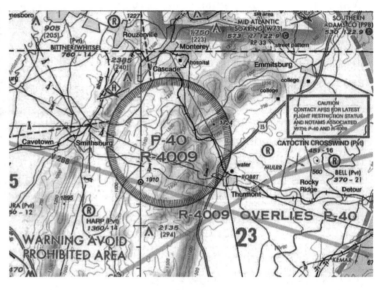

Figure 2-2. *An example of a prohibited area, P-40 around Camp David.*

Restricted Areas

Restricted areas are areas where operations are hazardous to nonparticipating aircraft and contain airspace within which the flight of aircraft, while not wholly prohibited, is subject to restrictions. Activities within these areas must be confined because of their nature, or limitations may be imposed upon aircraft operations that are not a part of those activities, or both. Restricted areas denote the existence of unusual, often invisible, hazards to aircraft (e.g., artillery firing, aerial gunnery, or guided missiles). Penetration of restricted areas without authorization from the using or controlling agency may be extremely hazardous to the aircraft.

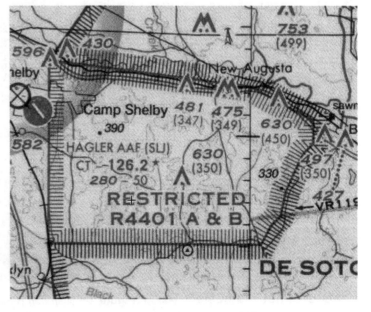

Figure 2-3. *Restricted areas on a sectional chart.*

1. If the restricted area is not active and has been released to the FAA, the ATC facility allows the aircraft to operate in the restricted airspace without issuing specific clearance for it to do so.
2. If the restricted area is active and has not been released to the FAA, the ATC facility issues a clearance that ensures the aircraft avoids the restricted airspace.

Restricted areas are charted with an "R" followed by a number (e.g., R-4401) and are depicted on the en route chart appropriate for use at the altitude or flight level (FL) being flown. *[Figure 10-1]* Restricted area information can be obtained on the back of the chart.

Warning Areas

Warning areas are similar in nature to restricted areas; however, the United States government does not have sole jurisdiction over the airspace. A warning area is airspace of defined dimensions, extending from 3 NM outward from the coast of the United States, containing activity that may be hazardous to nonparticipating aircraft. The purpose of such areas is to warn nonparticipating pilots of the potential danger. A warning area may be located over domestic or international waters or both. The airspace is designated with a "W" followed by a number (e.g., W-237). *[Figure 2-4]*

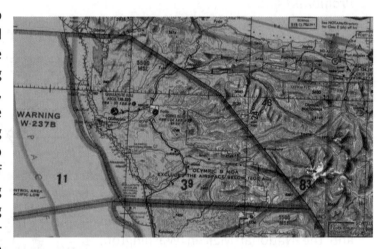

Figure 2-4. *Requirements for airspace operations.*

Military Operation Areas (MOAs)

MOAs consist of airspace with defined vertical and lateral limits established for the purpose of separating certain military training activities from IFR traffic. Whenever an MOA is being used, nonparticipating IFR traffic may be cleared through an MOA if IFR separation can be provided by ATC. Otherwise, ATC reroutes or restricts nonparticipating IFR traffic. MOAs are depicted on sectional, VFR terminal area, and en route low altitude charts and are not numbered (e.g., "Camden Ridge MOA"). *[Figure 2-5]* However, the MOA

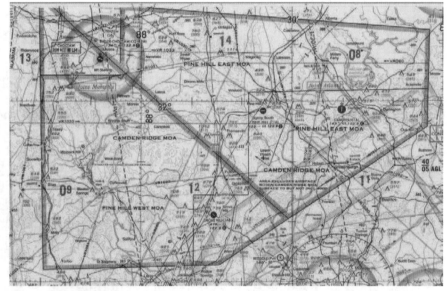

Figure 2-5. *Camden Ridge MOA is an example of a military operations area.*

is also further defined on the back of the sectional charts with times of operation, altitudes affected, and the controlling agency.

Alert Areas

Alert areas are depicted on aeronautical charts with an "A" followed by a number (e.g., A-211) to inform nonparticipating pilots of areas that may contain a high volume of pilot training or an unusual type of aerial activity. Pilots should exercise caution in alert areas. All activity within an alert area shall be conducted in accordance with regulations, without waiver, and pilots of participating aircraft, as well as pilots transiting the area, shall be equally responsible for collision avoidance. [Figure 2-6]

Figure 2-6. *Alert area (A-211).*

Controlled Firing Areas (CFAs)

CFAs contain activities that, if not conducted in a controlled environment, could be hazardous to nonparticipating aircraft. The difference between CFAs and other special use airspace is that activities must be suspended when a spotter aircraft, radar, or ground lookout position indicates an aircraft might be approaching the area. There is no need to chart CFAs since they do not cause a nonparticipating aircraft to change its flight path.

Other Airspace Areas

"Other airspace areas" is a general term referring to the majority of the remaining airspace. It includes:

- Local airport advisory (LAA)
- Military training route (MTR)
- Temporary flight restriction (TFR)
- Parachute jump aircraft operations
- Published VFR routes
- Terminal radar service area (TRSA)
- National security area (NSA)
- Air Defense Identification Zones (ADIZ) land and water based and need for Defense VFR (DVFR) flight plan to operate VFR in this airspace
- Flight Restricted Zones (FRZ) in vicinity of Capitol and White House

- Wildlife Areas/Wilderness Areas/National Parks and request to operate above 2,000 AGL
- National Oceanic and Atmospheric Administration (NOAA) Marine Areas off the coast with requirement to operate above 2,000 AGL
- Tethered Balloons for observation and weather recordings that extend on cables up to 60,000

Local Airport Advisory (LAA)

An advisory service provided by Flight Service facilities, which are located on the landing airport, using a discrete ground-to-air frequency or the tower frequency when the tower is closed. LAA services include local airport advisories, automated weather reporting with voice broadcasting, and a continuous Automated Surface Observing System (ASOS)/Automated Weather Observing Station (AWOS) data display, other continuous direct reading instruments, or manual observations available to the specialist.

Military Training Routes (MTRs)

MTRs are routes used by military aircraft to maintain proficiency in tactical flying. These routes are usually established below 10,000 feet MSL for operations at speeds in excess of 250 knots. Some route segments may be defined at higher altitudes for purposes of route continuity. Routes are identified as IFR (IR), and VFR (VR), followed by a number. *[Figure 2-7]* MTRs with no segment above 1,500 feet AGL are identified by four number characters (e.g., IR1206, VR1207). MTRs that include one or more segments above 1,500 feet AGL are identified by three number characters (e.g., IR206, VR207). IFR low altitude en route charts depict all IR routes and all VR routes that accommodate operations above 1,500 feet AGL. IR routes are conducted in accordance with IFR regardless of weather conditions. VFR sectional charts depict military training activities, such as IR, VR, MOA, restricted area, warning area, and alert area information.

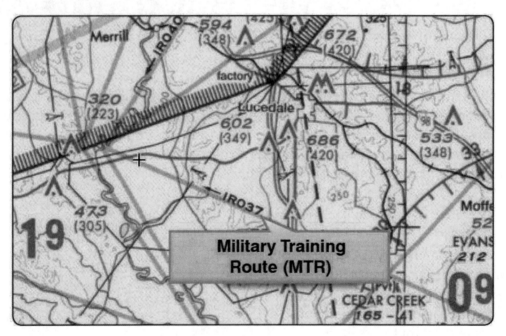

Figure 2-7. *Military training route (MTR) chart symbols.*

Temporary Flight Restrictions (TFR)

A flight data center (FDC) Notice to Airmen (NOTAM) is issued to designate a TFR. The NOTAM begins with the phrase "FLIGHT RESTRICTIONS" followed by the location of the temporary restriction, effective time period, area defined in statute miles, and altitudes affected. The NOTAM also contains the FAA coordination facility and telephone number, the reason for the restriction, and any other information deemed appropriate. The pilot should check the NOTAMs as part of flight planning.

Some of the purposes for establishing a TFR are:

- Protect persons and property in the air or on the surface from an existing or imminent hazard.
- Provide a safe environment for the operation of disaster relief aircraft.
- Prevent an unsafe congestion of sightseeing aircraft above an incident or event, that may generate a high degree of public interest.
- Protect declared national disasters for humanitarian reasons in the State of Hawaii.
- Protect the President, Vice President, or other public figures.
- Provide a safe environment for space agency operations.

Since the events of September 11, 2001, the use of TFRs has become much more common. There have been a number of incidents of aircraft incursions into TFRs that have resulted in pilots undergoing security investigations and certificate suspensions. It is a pilot's responsibility to be aware of TFRs in their proposed area of flight. One way to check is to visit the FAA website, www.tfr.faa.gov, and verify that there is not a TFR in the area.

Parachute Jump Aircraft Operations

Parachute jump aircraft operations are published in the Chart Supplement U.S. (formerly Airport/Facility Directory). Sites that are used frequently are depicted on sectional charts.

Published VFR Routes

Published VFR routes are for transitioning around, under, or through some complex airspace. Terms such as VFR flyway, VFR corridor, Class B airspace VFR transition route, and terminal area VFR route have been applied to such routes. These routes are generally found on VFR terminal area planning charts.

Terminal Radar Service Areas (TRSAs)

TRSAs are areas where participating pilots can receive additional radar services. The purpose of the service is to provide separation between all IFR operations and participating VFR aircraft.

The primary airport(s) within the TRSA become(s) Class D airspace. The remaining portion of the TRSA overlies other controlled airspace, which is normally Class E airspace beginning at 700 or 1,200 feet and established to transition to/ from the en route/terminal environment. TRSAs are depicted on VFR sectional charts and terminal area charts with a solid black line and altitudes for each segment. The Class D portion is charted with a blue segmented line. Participation in TRSA services is voluntary; however, pilots operating under VFR are encouraged to contact the radar approach control and take advantage of TRSA service.

National Security Areas (NSAs)

NSAs consist of airspace of defined vertical and lateral dimensions established at locations where there is a requirement for increased security and safety of ground facilities. Flight in NSAs may be temporarily prohibited by regulation under the provisions of Title 14 of the Code of Federal Regulations (14 CFR) part 99 and prohibitions are disseminated via NOTAM. Pilots are requested to voluntarily avoid flying through these depicted areas.

Air Traffic Control and the National Airspace System

The primary purpose of the ATC system is to prevent a collision between aircraft operating in the system and to organize and expedite the flow of traffic. In addition to its primary function, the ATC system has the capability to provide (with certain limitations) additional services. The ability to provide additional services is limited by many factors, such as the volume of traffic, frequency congestion, quality of radar, controller workload, higher priority duties, and the pure physical inability to scan and detect those situations that fall in this category. It is recognized that these services cannot be provided in cases in which the provision of services is precluded by the above factors.

Consistent with the aforementioned conditions, controllers shall provide additional service procedures to the extent permitted by higher priority duties and other circumstances. The provision of additional services is not optional on the part of the controller, but rather is required when the work situation permits. Provide ATC service in accordance with the procedures and minima in this order except when other procedures/minima are prescribed in a letter of agreement, FAA directive, or a military document.

Operating Rules and Pilot/Equipment Requirements

The safety of flight is a top priority of all pilots and the responsibilities associated with operating an aircraft should always be taken seriously. The air traffic system maintains a high degree of safety and efficiency with strict regulatory oversight of the FAA. Pilots fly in accordance with regulations that have served the United States well, as evidenced by the fact that the country has the safest aviation system in the world.

All aircraft operating in today's National Airspace System (NAS) has complied with the CFR governing its certification and maintenance; all pilots operating today have completed rigorous pilot certification training and testing. Of equal importance is the proper execution of preflight planning, aeronautical decision-making (ADM) and risk management. ADM involves a systematic approach to risk assessment and stress management in aviation, illustrates how personal attitudes can influence decision-making, and how those attitudes can be modified to enhance safety. More detailed information regarding ADM and risk mitigation can be found in <u>Chapter 10</u>, "Aeronautical Decision-Making and Judgment," of this study guide.

Pilots also comply with very strict FAA general operating and flight rules as outlined in the CFR, including the FAA's important "see and avoid" mandate. These regulations provide the historical foundation of the FAA regulations governing the aviation system and the individual classes of airspace.

Visual Flight Rules (VFR) Terms & Symbols

Remote pilots need to be familiar with the following information from the <u>FAA Aeronautical Chart User's Guide</u> website:

- All information on the *VFR Terms* tab
- The following sections under "VFR Aeronautical Chart Symbols" on the *VFR Symbols* tab:
  o Airports
  o Airspace Information
  o Navigational and Procedural Information
  o Chart Limits
  o Culture

o   Hydrography
o   Relief

Notices to Airmen (NOTAMs)

Notices to Airmen, or NOTAMs, are time-critical aeronautical information either temporary in nature or not sufficiently known in advance to permit publication on aeronautical charts or in other operational publications. The information receives immediate dissemination via the National Notice to Airmen (NOTAM) System. NOTAMs contain current notices to airmen that are considered essential to the safety of flight, as well as supplemental data affecting other operational publications. There are many different reasons that NOTAMs are issued. Following are some of those reasons:

- Hazards, such as air shows, parachute jumps, kite flying, and rocket launches
- Flights by important people such as heads of state
- Inoperable lights on tall obstructions
- Temporary erection of obstacles near airfields
- Passage of flocks of birds through airspace (a NOTAM in this category is known as a BIRDTAM)

NOTAMs are available in printed form through subscription from the Superintendent of Documents or online at PilotWeb, which provides access to current NOTAM information. Local airport NOTAMs can be obtained online from various websites. Some examples are www.fltplan.com and www.aopa.org/whatsnew/notams.html. Most sites require a free registration and acceptance of terms but offer pilots updated NOTAMs and TFRs.

This page intentionally left blank.

Chapter 3a:
Aviation Weather Sources

Introduction

In aviation, weather service is a combined effort of the National Weather Service (NWS), Federal Aviation Administration (FAA), Department of Defense (DOD), other aviation groups, and individuals. Because of the increasing need for worldwide weather services, foreign weather organizations also provide vital input. While weather forecasts are not 100 percent accurate, meteorologists, through careful scientific study and computer modeling, have the ability to predict weather patterns, trends, and characteristics with increasing accuracy. Through a complex system of weather services, government agencies, and independent weather observers, pilots and other aviation professionals receive the benefit of this vast knowledge base in the form of up-to-date weather reports and forecasts. These reports and forecasts enable pilots to make informed decisions regarding weather and flight safety before and during a flight.

Surface Aviation Weather Observations

Surface aviation weather observations are a compilation of elements of the current weather at individual ground stations across the United States. The network is made up of government and privately contracted facilities that provide continuous up-to-date weather information. Automated weather sources, such as the Automated Weather Observing Systems (AWOS), Automated Surface Observing Systems (ASOS), as well as other automated facilities, also play a major role in the gathering of surface observations.

Surface observations provide local weather conditions and other relevant information for a specific airport. This information includes the type of report, station identifier, date and time, modifier (as required), wind, visibility, runway visual range (RVR), weather phenomena, sky condition, temperature/dew point, altimeter reading, and applicable remarks. The information gathered for the surface observation may be from a person, an automated station, or an automated station that is updated or enhanced by a weather observer. In any form, the surface observation provides valuable information about individual airports around the country. These reports cover a small area and will be beneficial to the remote pilot.

Aviation Weather Reports

Aviation weather reports are designed to give accurate depictions of current weather conditions. Each report provides current information that is updated at different times. Some typical reports are METARs and PIREPs. To view a weather report, go to http://www.aviationweather.gov/.

Aviation Routine Weather Report (METAR)

A METAR is an observation of current surface weather reported in a standard international format. METARs are issued on a regularly scheduled basis unless significant weather changes have occurred. A special METAR (SPECI) can be issued at any time between routine METAR reports.

Example: METAR KGGG 161753Z AUTO 14021G26KT 3/4SM +TSRA BR BKN008 OVC012CB 18/17 A2970 RMK PRESFR

A typical METAR report contains the following information in sequential order:

1. Type of report—there are two types of METAR reports. The first is the routine METAR report that is transmitted on a regular time interval. The second is the aviation selected SPECI. This is a special report that can be given at any time to update the METAR for rapidly changing weather conditions, aircraft mishaps, or other critical information.

2. Station identifier—a four-letter code as established by the International Civil Aviation Organization (ICAO). In the 48 contiguous states, a unique three-letter identifier is preceded by the letter "K." For example, Gregg County Airport in Longview, Texas, is identified by the letters "KGGG," K being the country designation and GGG being the airport identifier. In other regions of the world, including Alaska and Hawaii, the first two letters of the four-letter ICAO identifier indicate the region, country, or state. Alaska identifiers always begin with the letters "PA" and Hawaii identifiers always begin with the letters "PH." Station identifiers can be found by searching various websites such as DUATS and NOAA's Aviation Weather Aviation Digital Data Services (ADDS).

3. Date and time of report—depicted in a six-digit group (161753Z). The first two digits are the date. The last four digits are the time of the METAR/SPECI, which is always given in coordinated universal time (UTC). A "Z" is appended to the end of the time to denote the time is given in Zulu time (UTC) as opposed to local time.

4. Modifier—denotes that the METAR/SPECI came from an automated source or that the report was corrected. If the notation "AUTO" is listed in the METAR/SPECI, the report came from an automated source. It also lists "AO1" (for no precipitation discriminator) or "AO2" (with precipitation discriminator) in the "Remarks" section to indicate the type of precipitation sensors employed at the automated station. When the modifier "COR" is used, it identifies a corrected report sent out to replace an earlier report that contained an error (for example: METAR KGGG 161753Z COR).

5. Wind—reported with five digits (14021KT) unless the speed is greater than 99 knots, in which case the wind is reported with six digits. The first three digits indicate the direction the true wind is blowing from in tens of degrees. If the wind is variable, it is reported as "VRB." The last two digits indicate the speed of the wind in knots unless the wind is greater than 99 knots, in which case it is indicated by three digits. If the winds are gusting, the letter "G" follows the wind speed (G26KT). After the letter "G," the peak gust recorded is provided. If the wind direction varies more than 60° and the wind speed is greater than six knots, a separate group of numbers, separated by a "V," will indicate the extremes of the wind directions.

6. Visibility—the prevailing visibility (¾ SM) is reported in statute miles as denoted by the letters "SM." It is reported in both miles and fractions of miles. At times, runway visual range (RVR) is reported following the prevailing visibility. RVR is the distance a pilot can see down the runway in a moving aircraft. When RVR is reported, it is shown with an R, then the runway number followed by a slant, then the visual range in feet. For example, when the RVR is reported as R17L/1400FT, it translates to a visual range of 1,400 feet on runway 17 left.

7. Weather—can be broken down into two different categories: qualifiers and weather phenomenon (+TSRA BR). First, the qualifiers of intensity, proximity, and the descriptor of the weather are given. The intensity may be light (–), moderate ( ), or heavy (+). Proximity only depicts weather phenomena that are in the airport vicinity. The notation "VC" indicates a specific weather phenomenon is in the vicinity of five to ten miles from the airport. Descriptors are used to describe certain types of precipitation and obscurations. Weather

phenomena may be reported as being precipitation, obscurations, and other phenomena, such as squalls or funnel clouds. Descriptions of weather phenomena as they begin or end and hailstone size are also listed in the "Remarks" sections of the report. *[Figure 3-1]*

Qualifier		Weather Phenomena		
Intensity or Proximity 1	Descriptor 2	Precipitation 3	Obscuration 4	Other 5
– Light	**MI** Shallow	**DZ** Drizzle	**BR** Mist	**PO** Dust/sand whirls
Moderate (no qualifier)	**BC** Patches	**RA** Rain	**FG** Fog	**SQ** Squalls
+ Heavy	**DR** Low drifting	**SN** Snow	**FU** Smoke	**FC** Funnel cloud
VC in the vicinity	**BL** Blowing	**SG** Snow grains	**DU** Dust	**+FC** Tornado or waterspout
	SH Showers	**IC** Ice crystals (diamond dust)	**SA** Sand	**SS** Sandstorm
	TS Thunderstorms	**PL** Ice pellets	**HZ** Haze	**DS** Dust storm
	FZ Freezing	**GR** Hail	**PY** Spray	
	PR Partial	**GS** Small hail or snow pellets	**VA** Volcanic ash	
		UP *Unknown precipitation		

The weather groups are constructed by considering columns 1–5 in this table in sequence:
intensity, followed by descriptor, followed by weather phenomena (e.g., heavy rain showers(s) is coded as +SHRA).
* Automated stations only

Figure 3-1. *Descriptors and weather phenomena used in a typical METAR.*

8. Sky condition—always reported in the sequence of amount, height, and type or indefinite ceiling/height (vertical visibility) (BKN008 OVC012CB, VV003). The heights of the cloud bases are reported with a three-digit number in hundreds of feet AGL. Clouds above 12,000 feet are not detected or reported by an automated station. The types of clouds, specifically towering cumulus (TCU) or cumulonimbus (CB) clouds, are reported with their height. Contractions are used to describe the amount of cloud coverage and obscuring phenomena. The amount of sky coverage is reported in eighths of the sky from horizon to horizon. *[Figure 3-2]*

Sky Cover	Contraction
Less than ⅛ (Clear)	SKC, CLR, FEW
⅛–²⁄₈ (Few)	FEW
³⁄₈–⁴⁄₈ (Scattered)	SCT
⁵⁄₈–⁷⁄₈ (Broken)	BKN
⁸⁄₈ or (Overcast)	OVC

Figure 3-2. *Reportable contractions for sky condition.*

9. Temperature and dew point—the air temperature and dew point are always given in degrees Celsius (C) or (18/17). Temperatures below 0 °C are preceded by the letter "M" to indicate minus.

10. Altimeter setting—reported as inches of mercury ("Hg) in a four-digit number group (A2970). It is always preceded by the letter "A." Rising or falling pressure may also be denoted in the "Remarks" sections as "PRESRR" or "PRESFR," respectively.

11. Zulu time—a term used in aviation for UTC, which places the entire world on one time standard.

12. Remarks—the remarks section always begins with the letters "RMK." Comments may or may not appear in this section of the METAR. The information contained in this section may include wind data, variable visibility, beginning and ending times of particular phenomenon, pressure information, and various other information deemed necessary. An example of a remark regarding weather phenomenon that does not fit in any other category would be: OCNL LTGICCG. This translates as occasional lightning in the clouds and from cloud to ground. Automated stations also use the remarks section to indicate the equipment needs maintenance.

Example: METAR KGGG 161753Z AUTO 14021G26KT 3/4SM +TSRA BR BKN008 OVC012CB 18/17 A2970 RMK PRESFR

Explanation: Routine METAR for Gregg County Airport for the 16th day of the month at 1753Z automated source. Winds are 140 at 21 knots gusting to 26. Visibility is ¾ statute mile. Thunderstorms with heavy rain and mist. Ceiling is broken at 800 feet, overcast at 1,200 feet with cumulonimbus clouds. Temperature 18 °C and dew point 17 °C. Barometric pressure is 29.70 "Hg and falling rapidly.

Aviation Forecasts

Observed weather condition reports are often used in the creation of forecasts for the same area. A variety of different forecast products are produced and designed to be used in the preflight planning stage. The printed forecasts that pilots need to be familiar with are the terminal aerodrome forecast (TAF), aviation area forecast (FA), inflight weather advisories (Significant Meteorological Information (SIGMET), Airman's Meteorological Information (AIRMET)), and the winds and temperatures aloft forecast (FB).

Terminal Aerodrome Forecasts (TAF)

A TAF is a report established for the five statute mile radius around an airport. TAF reports are usually given for larger airports. Each TAF is valid for a 24 or 30-hour time period and is updated four times a day at 0000Z, 0600Z, 1200Z, and 1800Z. The TAF utilizes the same descriptors and abbreviations as used in the METAR report. These weather reports can be beneficial to the remote pilot for flight planning purposes. The TAF includes the following information in sequential order:

1. Type of report—a TAF can be either a routine forecast (TAF) or an amended forecast (TAF AMD).
2. ICAO station identifier—the station identifier is the same as that used in a METAR.
3. Date and time of origin—time and date (081125Z) of TAF origination is given in the six-number code with the first two being the date, the last four being the time. Time is always given in UTC as denoted by the Z following the time block.
4. Valid period dates and times—The TAF valid period (0812/0912) follows the date/time of forecast origin group. Scheduled 24 and 30 hour TAFs are issued four times per day, at 0000, 0600, 1200, and 1800Z. The first two digits (08) are the day of the month for the start of the TAF. The next two digits (12) are the starting hour (UTC). 09 is the day of the month for the end of the TAF, and the last two digits (12) are the ending hour (UTC) of the valid period. A forecast period that begins at midnight UTC is annotated as 00. If the end time of a valid

period is at midnight UTC, it is annotated as 24. For example, a 00Z TAF issued on the 9th of the month and valid for 24 hours would have a valid period of 0900/0924.

5. Forecast wind—the wind direction and speed forecast are coded in a five-digit number group. An example would be 15011KT. The first three digits indicate the direction of the wind in reference to true north. The last two digits state the wind speed in knots appended with "KT." Like the METAR, winds greater than 99 knots are given in three digits.

6. Forecast visibility—given in statute miles and may be in whole numbers or fractions. If the forecast is greater than six miles, it is coded as "P6SM."

7. Forecast significant weather—weather phenomena are coded in the TAF reports in the same format as the METAR.

8. Forecast sky condition—given in the same format as the METAR. Only CB clouds are forecast in this portion of the TAF report as opposed to CBs and towering cumulus in the METAR.

9. Forecast change group—for any significant weather change forecast to occur during the TAF time period, the expected conditions and time period are included in this group. This information may be shown as from (FM), and temporary (TEMPO). "FM" is used when a rapid and significant change, usually within an hour, is expected. "TEMPO" is used for temporary fluctuations of weather, expected to last less than 1 hour.

10. PROB30—a given percentage that describes the probability of thunderstorms and precipitation occurring in the coming hours. This forecast is not used for the first 6 hours of the 24-hour forecast.

Example: TAF KPIR 111130Z 1112/1212 TEMPO 1112/1114 5SM BR FM1500 16015G25KT P6SM SCT040 BKN250 FM120000 14012KT P6SM BKN080 OVC150 PROB30 1200/1204 3SM TSRA BKN030CB FM120400 1408KT P6SM SCT040 OVC080 TEMPO 1204/1208 3SM TSRA OVC030CB

Explanation: Routine TAF for Pierre, South Dakota...on the 11th day of the month, at 1130Z...valid for 24 hours from 1200Z on the 11th to 1200Z on the 12th...wind from 150° at 12 knots... visibility greater than 6 SM...broken clouds at 9,000 feet... temporarily, between 1200Z and 1400Z, visibility 5 SM in mist...from 1500Z winds from 160° at 15 knots, gusting to 25 knots visibility greater than 6 SM...clouds scattered at 4,000 feet and broken at 25,000 feet...from 0000Z wind from 140° at 12 knots...visibility greater than 6 SM...clouds broken at 8,000 feet, overcast at 15,000 feet...between 0000Z and 0400Z, there is 30 percent probability of visibility 3 SM...thunderstorm with moderate rain showers...clouds broken at 3,000 feet with cumulonimbus clouds...from 0400Z...winds from 140° at 8 knots...visibility greater than 6 miles...clouds at 4,000 scattered and overcast at 8,000... temporarily between 0400Z and 0800Z...visibility 3 miles... thunderstorms with moderate rain showers...clouds overcast at 3,000 feet with cumulonimbus clouds...end of report (=).

Convective Significant Meteorological Information (WST)

Convective SIGMETs are issued for severe thunderstorms with surface winds greater than 50 knots, hail at the surface greater than or equal to ¾ inch in diameter, or tornadoes. They are also issued to advise pilots of embedded thunderstorms, lines of thunderstorms, or thunderstorms with heavy or greater precipitation that affect 40 percent or more of a 3,000 square mile or greater region. A remote pilot will find these weather alerts helpful for flight planning.

This page intentionally left blank.

Chapter 3b:
Effects of Weather on Small Unmanned Aircraft Performance

Introduction

This chapter discusses the factors that affect aircraft performance, which include the aircraft weight, atmospheric conditions, runway environment, and the fundamental physical laws governing the forces acting on an aircraft.

Since the characteristics of the atmosphere have a major effect on performance, it is necessary to review two dominant factors—pressure and temperature.

Density Altitude

The more appropriate term for correlating aerodynamic performance in the nonstandard atmosphere is density altitude—the altitude in the standard atmosphere corresponding to a particular value of air density.

As the density of the air increases (lower density altitude), aircraft performance increases. Conversely, as air density decreases (higher density altitude), aircraft performance decreases. A decrease in air density means a high density altitude; an increase in air density means a lower density altitude. Density altitude has a direct effect on aircraft performance.

Air density is affected by changes in altitude, temperature, and humidity. High density altitude refers to thin air while low density altitude refers to dense air. The conditions that result in a high density altitude are high elevations, low atmospheric pressures, high temperatures, high humidity, or some combination of these factors. Lower elevations, high atmospheric pressure, low temperatures, and low humidity are more indicative of low density altitude.

Effects of Pressure on Density

Since air is a gas, it can be compressed or expanded. When air is compressed, a greater amount of air can occupy a given volume. Conversely, when pressure on a given volume of air is decreased, the air expands and occupies a greater space. That is, the original column of air at a lower pressure contains a smaller mass of air. In other words, the density is decreased. In fact, density is directly proportional to pressure. If the pressure is doubled, the density is doubled, and if the pressure is lowered, so is the density. This statement is true only at a constant temperature.

Effects of Temperature on Density

Increasing the temperature of a substance decreases its density. Conversely, decreasing the temperature increases the density. Thus, the density of air varies inversely with temperature. This statement is true only at a constant pressure.

In the atmosphere, both temperature and pressure decrease with altitude and have conflicting effects upon density. However, the fairly rapid drop in pressure as altitude is increased usually has the dominant effect. Hence, pilots can expect the density to decrease with altitude.

Effects of Humidity (Moisture) on Density

The preceding paragraphs are based on the presupposition of perfectly dry air. In reality, it is never completely dry. The small amount of water vapor suspended in the atmosphere may be negligible under certain conditions, but in other conditions humidity may become an important factor in the performance of an aircraft. Water vapor is lighter than air; consequently, moist air is lighter than dry air. Therefore, as the water content of the air increases, the air becomes less dense, increasing density altitude and decreasing performance. It is lightest or least dense when, in a given set of conditions, it contains the maximum amount of water vapor.

Humidity, also called relative humidity, refers to the amount of water vapor contained in the atmosphere and is expressed as a percentage of the maximum amount of water vapor the air can hold. This amount varies with the temperature; warm air can hold more water vapor, while colder air can hold less. Perfectly dry air that contains no water vapor has a relative humidity of zero percent, while saturated air that cannot hold any more water vapor has a relative humidity of 100 percent. Humidity alone is usually not considered an essential factor in calculating density altitude and aircraft performance; however, it does contribute.

Performance

Performance is a term used to describe the ability of an aircraft to accomplish certain things that make it useful for certain purposes.

The primary factors most affected by performance are the takeoff and landing distance, rate of climb, ceiling, payload, range, speed, maneuverability, stability, and fuel economy.

Climb Performance Factors

Since weight, altitude and configuration changes affect excess thrust and power, they also affect climb performance. Climb performance is directly dependent upon the ability to produce either excess thrust or excess power.

Weight has a very pronounced effect on aircraft performance. If weight is added to an aircraft, it must fly at a higher angle of attack (AOA) to maintain a given altitude and speed. This increases the induced drag of the wings, as well as the parasite drag of the aircraft. Increased drag means that additional thrust is needed to overcome it, which in turn means that less reserve thrust is available for climbing. Aircraft designers go to great lengths to minimize the weight, since it has such a marked effect on the factors pertaining to performance.

A change in an aircraft's weight produces a twofold effect on climb performance. An increase in altitude also increases the power required and decreases the power available. Therefore, the climb performance of an aircraft diminishes with altitude.

Measurement of Atmosphere Pressure

To provide a common reference, the International Standard Atmosphere (ISA) has been established. These standard conditions are the basis for most aircraft performance data. Standard sea level pressure is defined as 29.92 "Hg and a standard temperature of 59 °F (15 °C). Atmospheric pressure is also reported in millibars (mb), with 1 "Hg equal to approximately 34 mb. Standard sea level pressure is 1,013.2 mb. Typical mb pressure readings range from 950.0 to 1,040.0 mb. Surface charts, high and low pressure centers, and hurricane data are reported using mb.

Since weather stations are located around the globe, all local barometric pressure readings are converted to a sea level pressure to provide a standard for records and reports. To achieve this, each station converts its barometric pressure by adding approximately 1 "Hg for every 1,000 feet of elevation. For example, a station at 5,000 feet above sea level, with a reading of 24.92 "Hg, reports a sea level pressure reading of 29.92 "Hg.

By tracking barometric pressure trends across a large area, weather forecasters can more accurately predict movement of pressure systems and the associated weather. For example, tracking a pattern of rising pressure at a single weather station generally indicates the approach of fair weather. Conversely, decreasing or rapidly falling pressure usually indicates approaching bad weather and, possibly, severe storms.

Effect of Obstructions on Wind

Another atmospheric hazard exists that can create problems for pilots. Obstructions on the ground affect the flow of wind and can be an unseen danger. Ground topography and large buildings can break up the flow of the wind and create wind gusts that change rapidly in direction and speed. These obstructions range from man-made structures, like hangars, to large natural obstructions, such as mountains, bluffs, or canyons.

The intensity of the turbulence associated with ground obstructions depends on the size of the obstacle and the primary velocity of the wind. This can affect the performance of any aircraft and can present a very serious hazard.

This same condition is even more noticeable when flying in mountainous regions. *[Figure 3-3]* While the wind flows smoothly up the windward side of the mountain and the upward currents help to carry an aircraft over the peak of the mountain, the wind on the leeward side does not act in a similar manner. As the air flows down the leeward side of the mountain, the air follows the contour of the terrain and is increasingly turbulent. This tends to push an aircraft into the side of a mountain. The stronger the wind, the greater the downward pressure and turbulence become.

Figure 3-3. *Turbulence in mountainous regions.*

Low-Level Wind Shear

Wind shear is a sudden, drastic change in wind speed and/or direction over a very small area. Wind shear can subject an aircraft to violent updrafts and downdrafts, as well as abrupt changes to the horizontal movement of the aircraft. While wind shear can occur at any altitude, low-level wind shear is especially hazardous due to the proximity of an aircraft to the ground. Low-level wind shear is commonly associated with passing frontal systems, thunderstorms, temperature inversions, and strong upper level winds (greater than 25 knots).

Wind shear is dangerous to an aircraft. It can rapidly change the performance of the aircraft and disrupt the normal flight attitude. For example, a tailwind quickly changing to a headwind causes an increase in airspeed and performance. Conversely, a headwind changing to a tailwind causes a decrease in airspeed and performance. In either case, a pilot must be prepared to react immediately to these changes to maintain control of the aircraft.

The most severe type of low-level wind shear, a microburst, is associated with convective precipitation into dry air at cloud base. Microburst activity may be indicated by an intense rain shaft at the surface but virga at cloud base and a ring of blowing dust is often the only visible clue. A typical microburst has a horizontal diameter of 1–2 miles and a nominal depth of 1,000 feet. The lifespan of a microburst is about 5–15 minutes during which time it can produce downdrafts of up to 6,000 feet per minute (fpm) and headwind losses of 30–90 knots, seriously degrading performance. It can also produce strong turbulence and hazardous wind direction changes. During an inadvertent microburst encounter, the small UA may first experience a performance-increasing headwind, followed by performance-decreasing downdrafts, followed by a rapidly increasing tailwind. This can result in terrain impact or flight dangerously close to the ground. An encounter during approach involves the same sequence of wind changes and could force the small UA to the ground short of the intended landing area.

It is important to remember that wind shear can affect any flight at any altitude. While wind shear may be reported, it often remains undetected and is a silent danger to aviation. Always be alert to the possibility of wind shear, especially when flying in and around thunderstorms and frontal systems.

Atmospheric Stability

The stability of the atmosphere depends on its ability to resist vertical motion. A stable atmosphere makes vertical movement difficult, and small vertical disturbances dampen out and disappear. In an unstable atmosphere, small vertical air movements tend to become larger, resulting in turbulent airflow and convective activity. Instability can lead to significant turbulence, extensive vertical clouds, and severe weather.

The combination of moisture and temperature determine the stability of the air and the resulting weather. Cool, dry air is very stable and resists vertical movement, which leads to good and generally clear weather. The greatest instability occurs when the air is moist and warm, as it is in the tropical regions in the summer. Typically, thunderstorms appear on a daily basis in these regions due to the instability of the surrounding air.

Inversion

As air rises and expands in the atmosphere, the temperature decreases. There is an atmospheric anomaly that can occur; however, that changes this typical pattern of atmospheric behavior. When the temperature of the air rises with altitude, a temperature inversion exists. Inversion layers are commonly shallow layers of smooth, stable air close to the ground. The temperature of the air increases with altitude to a certain point, which is the top of the inversion. The air at the top of the layer acts as a lid, keeping weather and pollutants trapped below. If the relative humidity of the air is high, it can contribute to the formation of clouds, fog, haze, or smoke resulting in diminished visibility in the inversion layer.

Surface-based temperature inversions occur on clear, cool nights when the air close to the ground is cooled by the lowering temperature of the ground. The air within a few hundred feet of the surface becomes cooler than the air above it. Frontal inversions occur when warm air spreads over a layer of cooler air, or cooler air is forced under a layer of warmer air.

Temperature/Dew Point Relationship

The relationship between dew point and temperature defines the concept of relative humidity. The dew point, given in degrees, is the temperature at which the air can hold no more moisture. When the temperature of the air is reduced to the dew point, the air is completely saturated and moisture begins to condense out of the air in the form of fog, dew, frost, clouds, rain, or snow.

Methods by Which Air Reaches the Saturation Point

If air reaches the saturation point while temperature and dew point are close together, it is highly likely that fog, low clouds, and precipitation will form. There are four methods by which air can reach the saturation point. First, when warm air moves over a cold surface, the air temperature drops and reaches the saturation point. Second, the saturation point may be reached when cold air and warm air mix. Third, when air cools at night through contact with the cooler ground, air reaches its saturation point. The fourth method occurs when air is lifted or is forced upward in the atmosphere.

Dew and Frost

On cool, clear, calm nights, the temperature of the ground and objects on the surface can cause temperatures of the surrounding air to drop below the dew point. When this occurs, the moisture in the air condenses and deposits itself on the ground, buildings, and other objects like cars and aircraft. This moisture is known as dew and sometimes can be seen on grass and other objects in the morning. If the temperature is below freezing, the moisture is deposited in the form of frost. While dew poses no threat to a small UA, frost poses a definite flight safety hazard. Frost disrupts the flow of air over the wing and can drastically reduce the production of lift. It also increases drag, which when combined with lowered lift production, can adversely affect the ability to take off. A small UA must be thoroughly cleaned and free of frost prior to beginning a flight.

Clouds

To pilots, the cumulonimbus cloud is perhaps the most dangerous cloud type. It appears individually or in groups and is known as either an air mass or orographic thunderstorm. Heating of the air near the Earth's surface creates an air mass thunderstorm; the upslope motion of air in the mountainous regions causes orographic thunderstorms. Cumulonimbus clouds that form in a continuous line are nonfrontal bands of thunderstorms or squall lines.

Since rising air currents cause cumulonimbus clouds, they are extremely turbulent and pose a significant hazard to flight safety. For example, if a small UA enters a thunderstorm, the small UA could experience updrafts and downdrafts that exceed 3,000 fpm. In addition, thunderstorms can produce large hailstones, damaging lightning, tornadoes, and large quantities of water, all of which are potentially hazardous to an aircraft.

Standing Lenticular Altocumulus Clouds.

Standing lenticular altocumulus clouds are formed on the crests of waves created by barriers in the wind flow. The clouds show little movement, hence the name *standing*. Wind, however, can be quite strong blowing through such clouds. They are characterized by their smooth, polished edges. The presence of these clouds is a good indication of very strong turbulence and should be avoided.

Stability

Stability of an air mass determines its typical weather characteristics. When one type of air mass overlies another, conditions change with height. Characteristics typical of an unstable and a stable air mass are as follows:

Unstable Air	Stable Air
Cumuliform clouds	Stratiform clouds and fog
Showery precipitation	Continuous precipitation
Rough air (turbulence)	Smooth air
Good visibility (except in blowing obstructions)	Fair to poor visibility in haze and smoke

Fronts

As air masses move out of their source regions, they come in contact with other air masses of different properties. The zone between two different air masses is a frontal zone or front. Across this zone, temperature, humidity and wind often change rapidly over short distances.

Mountain Flying

When planning a flight over mountainous terrain, gather as much preflight information as possible on cloud reports, wind direction, wind speed, and stability of air. Satellites often help locate mountain waves. Adequate information may not always be available, so remain alert for signposts in the sky.

Wind at mountain top level in excess of 25 knots suggests some turbulence. Wind in excess of 40 knots across a mountain barrier dictates caution. Stratified clouds mean stable air. Standing lenticular and/or rotor clouds suggest a mountain wave; expect turbulence many miles to the lee of mountains and relative smooth flight on the windward side. Convective clouds on the windward side of mountains mean unstable air; expect turbulence in close proximity to and on either side of the mountain.

Structural Icing

Two conditions are necessary for structural icing in flight:

1. The aircraft must be flying through visible water such as rain or cloud droplets
2. The temperature at the point where the moisture strikes the aircraft must be 0° C or colder.

Aerodynamic cooling can lower temperature of an airfoil to 0° C even though the ambient temperature is a few degrees warmer.

Thunderstorm Life Cycle

A thunderstorm cell during its life cycle progresses through three stages-(1) the cumulus, (2) the mature, and (3) the dissipating. It is virtually impossible to visually detect the transition from one stage to another; the transition is subtle and by no means abrupt. Furthermore, a thunderstorm may be a cluster of cells in different stages of the lifecycle.

The Cumulus Stage

Although most cumulus clouds do not grow into thunderstorms, every thunderstorm begins as a cumulus. The key feature of the cumulus stage is an updraft as illustrated in *figure 3-4*. The updraft varies in strength and extends from very near the surface to the cloud top. Growth rate of the cloud may exceed 3,000 feet per minute, so it is inadvisable to operate a small UA in an area of rapidly building cumulus clouds. Early during the cumulus stage, water droplets are quite small but grow to raindrop size as the cloud grows. The upwelling air carries the liquid water above the freezing level creating an icing hazard. As the raindrops grow still heavier, they fall. The cold rain drags air with it creating a cold downdraft coexisting with the updraft; the cell has reached the mature stage.

The Mature Stage

Precipitation beginning to fall from the cloud base is your signal that a downdraft has developed and a cell has entered the mature stage. Cold rain in the downdraft retards compressional heating, and the downdraft remains cooler than surrounding air. Therefore, its downward speed is accelerated and may exceed 2,500 feet per minute. The down rushing air spreads outward at the surface as shown in *figure 3-4* producing strong, gusty surface winds, a sharp temperature drop, and a rapid rise in pressure. The surface wind surge is a "plow wind" and its leading edge is the "first gust." Meanwhile, updrafts reach a maximum with speeds possibly exceeding 6,000 feet per minute. Updrafts and downdrafts in close proximity create strong vertical shear and a very turbulent environment. All thunderstorm hazards reach their greatest intensity during the mature stage.

The Dissipating Stage

Downdrafts characterize the dissipating stage of the thunderstorm cell as shown in *figure 3-4* and the storm dies rapidly. When rain has ended and downdrafts have abated, the dissipating stage 'is complete. When all cells of the thunderstorm have completed this stage, only harmless cloud remnants remain.

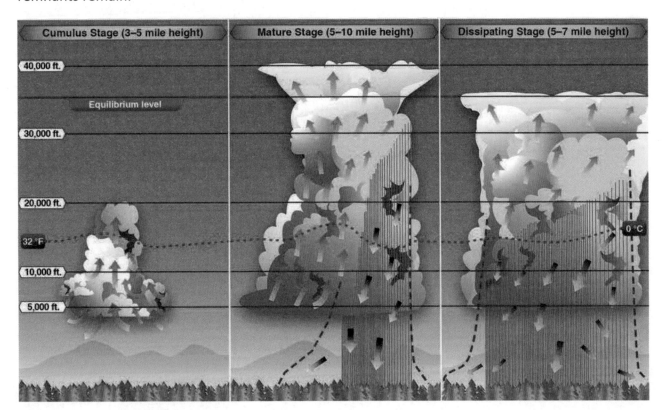

Figure 3-4. *Life cycle of a thunderstorm.*

Ceiling

For aviation purposes, a ceiling is the lowest layer of clouds reported as being broken or overcast, or the vertical visibility into an obscuration like fog or haze. Clouds are reported as broken when five-eighths to seven-eighths of the sky is covered with clouds. Overcast means the entire sky is covered with clouds. Current ceiling information is reported by the aviation routine weather report (METAR) and automated weather stations of various types.

Visibility

Closely related to cloud cover and reported ceilings is visibility information. Visibility refers to the greatest horizontal distance at which prominent objects can be viewed with the naked eye. Current visibility is also reported in METAR and other aviation weather reports, as well as by automated weather systems. Visibility information, as predicted by meteorologists, is available for a pilot during a preflight weather briefing.

Chapter 4:
Small Unmanned Aircraft Loading

Introduction

Before any flight, the remote pilot-in-command (PIC) should verify the aircraft is correctly loaded by determining the weight and balance condition of the aircraft. An aircraft's weight and balance restrictions established by the manufacturer or the builder should be closely followed. Compliance with the manufacturer's weight and balance limits is critical to flight safety. The remote PIC must consider the consequences of an overweight aircraft if an emergency condition arises.

- Although a maximum gross takeoff weight may be specified, the aircraft may not always safely take off with this load under all conditions. Conditions that affect takeoff and climb performance, such as high elevations, high air temperatures, and high humidity (high density altitudes) may require a reduction in weight before flight is attempted. Other factors to consider prior to takeoff are runway/launch area length, surface, slope, surface wind, and the presence of obstacles. These factors may require a reduction in weight prior to flight.
- Weight changes during flight also have a direct effect on aircraft performance. Fuel burn is the most common weight change that takes place during flight. As fuel is used, the aircraft becomes lighter and performance is improved, but this could have a negative effect on balance. In small UA operations, weight change during flight may occur when expendable items are used on board (e.g., a jettisonable load).

Adverse balance conditions (i.e., weight distribution) may affect flight characteristics in much the same manner as those mentioned for an excess weight condition. Limits for the location of the center of gravity (CG) may be established by the manufacturer. The CG is not a fixed point marked on the aircraft; its location depends on the distribution of aircraft weight. As variable load items are shifted or expended, there may be a resultant shift in CG location. The remote PIC should determine how the CG will shift and the resultant effects on the aircraft. If the CG is not within the allowable limits after loading or do not remain within the allowable limits for safe flight, it will be necessary to relocate or shed some weight before flight is attempted.

Weight

Gravity is the pulling force that tends to draw all bodies to the center of the earth. The CG may be considered as a point at which all the weight of the aircraft is concentrated. If the aircraft were supported at its exact CG, it would balance in any attitude. It will be noted that CG is of major importance in a small UA, for its position has a great bearing upon stability. The allowable location of the CG is determined by the general design of each particular aircraft. The designers determine how far the center of pressure (CP) will travel. It is important to understand that an aircraft's weight is concentrated at the CG and the aerodynamic forces of lift occur at the CP. When the CG is forward of the CP, there is a natural tendency for the aircraft to want to pitch nose down. If the CP is forward of the CG, a nose up pitching moment is created. Therefore, designers fix the aft limit of the CG forward of the CP for the corresponding flight speed in order to retain flight equilibrium.

Weight has a definite relationship to lift. This relationship is simple, but important in understanding the aerodynamics of flying. Lift is the upward force on the wing acting perpendicular to the relative wind and perpendicular to the aircraft's lateral axis. Lift is required to counteract the aircraft's weight. In stabilized level flight, when the lift force is equal to the weight force, the aircraft is in a state of equilibrium and neither accelerates upward or downward. If lift becomes less than weight, the vertical speed will decrease. When lift is greater than weight, the vertical speed will increase.

Stability

Stability is the inherent quality of an aircraft to correct for conditions that may disturb its equilibrium and to return to or to continue on the original flight path. It is primarily an aircraft design characteristic.

Stability in an aircraft affects two areas significantly:

- Maneuverability—the quality of an aircraft that permits it to be maneuvered easily and to withstand the stresses imposed by maneuvers. It is governed by the aircraft's weight, inertia, size and location of flight controls, structural strength, and powerplant. It too is an aircraft design characteristic.
- Controllability—the capability of an aircraft to respond to the pilot's control, especially with regard to flight path and attitude. It is the quality of the aircraft's response to the pilot's control application when maneuvering the aircraft, regardless of its stability characteristics.

Load Factors

In aerodynamics, the maximum load factor (at given bank angle) is a proportion between lift and weight and has a trigonometric relationship. The load factor is measured in Gs (acceleration of gravity), a unit of force equal to the force exerted by gravity on a body at rest and indicates the force to which a body is subjected when it is accelerated. Any force applied to an aircraft to deflect its flight from a straight line produces a stress on its structure. The amount of this force is the load factor. While a course in aerodynamics is not a prerequisite for obtaining a remote pilot certificate, the competent pilot should have a solid understanding of the forces that act on the aircraft, the advantageous use of these forces, and the operating limitations of the aircraft being flown.

For example, a load factor of 3 means the total load on an aircraft's structure is three times its weight. Since load factors are expressed in terms of Gs, a load factor of 3 may be spoken of as 3 Gs, or a load factor of 4 as 4 Gs.

With the structural design of aircraft planned to withstand only a certain amount of overload, a knowledge of load factors has become essential for all pilots. Load factors are important for two reasons:

1. It is possible for a pilot to impose a dangerous overload on the aircraft structures.
2. An increased load factor increases the stalling speed and makes stalls possible at seemingly safe flight speeds.

Load Factors in Steep Turns

At a constant altitude, during a coordinated turn in any aircraft, the load factor is the result of two forces: centrifugal force and weight. *[Figure 4-1]* For any given bank angle, the rate-of-turn varies with the airspeed—the higher the speed, the slower the rate-of-turn (ROT). This compensates for added centrifugal force, allowing the load factor to remain the same.

Figure 4-2 reveals an important fact about turns—the load factor increases at a terrific rate after a bank has reached 45° or 50°. The load factor for any aircraft in a coordinated level turn at 60° bank is 2 Gs. The load factor in an 80° bank is 5.76 Gs. The wing must produce lift equal to these load factors if altitude is to be maintained.

It should be noted how rapidly the line denoting load factor rises as it approaches the 90° bank line, which it never quite reaches because a 90° banked, constant altitude turn is not mathematically possible. An aircraft may be banked to 90° in a coordinated turn if not trying to hold altitude. An aircraft that can be held in a 90° banked slipping turn is capable of straight knife-edged flight. At slightly more than 80°, the load factor exceeds the limit of 6 Gs, the limit load factor of an acrobatic aircraft.

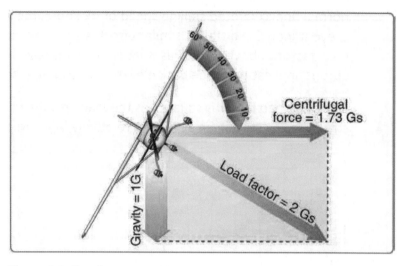

Figure 4-1. *Two forces cause load factor during turns.*

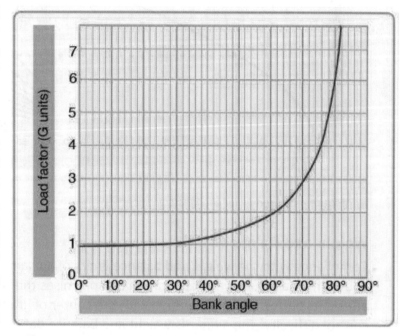

Figure 4-2. *Angle of bank changes load factor in level flight.*

Load Factors and Stalling Speeds

Any aircraft, within the limits of its structure, may be stalled at any airspeed. When a sufficiently high AOA is imposed, the smooth flow of air over an airfoil breaks up and separates, producing an abrupt change of flight characteristics and a sudden loss of lift, which results in a stall.

A study of this effect has revealed that an aircraft's stalling speed increases in proportion to the square root of the load factor. This means that an aircraft with a normal unaccelerated stalling speed of 50 knots can be stalled at 100 knots by inducing a load factor of 4 Gs. If it were possible for this aircraft to withstand a load factor of nine, it could be stalled at a speed of 150 knots. A pilot should be aware of the danger of inadvertently stalling the aircraft by increasing the load factor, as in a steep turn or spiral.

Figures 4-2 and 4-3 show that banking an aircraft greater than 72° in a steep turn produces a load factor of 3, and the stalling speed is increased significantly. If this turn is made in an aircraft with a normal unaccelerated stalling speed of 45 knots, the airspeed must be kept greater than 75 knots to prevent inducing a stall. A similar effect is experienced in a quick pull up or any maneuver producing load factors above 1 G. This sudden, unexpected loss of control, particularly in a steep turn or abrupt application of the back elevator control near the ground, has caused many accidents.

Since the load factor is squared as the stalling speed doubles, tremendous loads may be imposed on structures by stalling an aircraft at relatively high airspeeds.

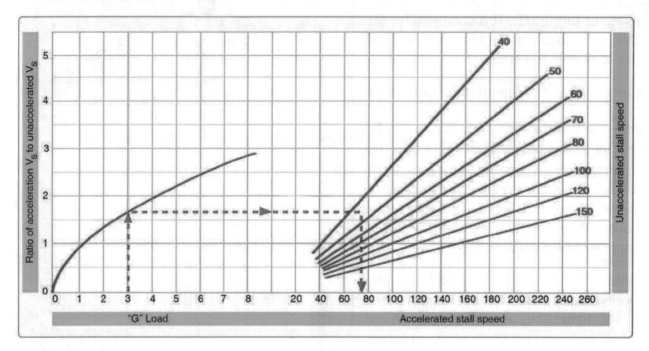

Figure 4-3. *Load factor changes stall speed.*

Weight and Balance

Compliance with the weight and balance limits of any aircraft is critical to flight safety. Operating above the maximum weight limitation compromises the structural integrity of an aircraft and adversely affects its performance. Operation with the center of gravity (CG) outside the approved limits results in control difficulty. The aircraft's weight and balance data is important information for a pilot that must be frequently reevaluated.

Weight Control

Weight is the force with which gravity attracts a body toward the center of the Earth. It is a product of the mass of a body and the acceleration acting on the body. Weight is a major factor in aircraft construction and operation and demands respect from all pilots. The force of gravity continuously attempts to pull an aircraft down toward Earth. The force of lift is the only force that counteracts weight and sustains an aircraft in flight. The amount of lift produced by an airfoil is limited by the airfoil design, AOA, airspeed, and air density. To assure that the lift generated is sufficient to counteract weight, loading an aircraft beyond the manufacturer's recommended weight must be avoided. If the weight is greater than the lift generated, the aircraft may be incapable of flight.

Effects of Weight

Any item aboard an aircraft that increases the total weight is undesirable for performance. Manufacturers attempt to make an aircraft as light as possible without sacrificing strength or safety.

The pilot should always be aware of the consequences of overloading. An overloaded aircraft may not be able to leave the ground, or if it does become airborne, it may exhibit unexpected and unusually poor flight characteristics. If not properly loaded, the initial indication of poor performance usually takes place during takeoff.

Excessive weight reduces the flight performance in almost every respect. For example, the most important performance deficiencies of an overloaded aircraft are:

- Higher takeoff speed
- Longer takeoff run
- Reduced rate and angle of climb
- Lower maximum altitude
- Shorter range
- Reduced cruising speed
- Reduced maneuverability
- Higher stalling speed
- Higher approach and landing speed
- Longer landing roll

The pilot must be knowledgeable about the effect of weight on the performance of the particular aircraft being flown. Excessive weight in itself reduces the safety margins available to the pilot and becomes even more hazardous when other performance-reducing factors are combined with excess weight. The pilot must also consider the consequences of an overweight aircraft if an emergency condition arises.

This page intentionally left blank.

Chapter 5:
Emergency Procedures

Introduction

An inflight emergency is usually an unexpected and unforeseen event that can have serious consequences for an unprepared remote pilot. During an emergency, a remote pilot is permitted to deviate from any part of 14 CFR part 107 to respond to the emergency. When a remote pilot does deviate from a rule due to an emergency, the remote will report the emergency if asked to do so by the FAA (also referred to as "the Administrator").

Inflight Emergency

A remote pilot is responsible for the safe operation of the small UA at all times. A remote pilot must ensure that the aircraft is in a safe operating condition before flight, that there is not any hazard to persons or property, and that all required crew members are properly briefed on the operation and emergency procedures.

Before every flight, a remote pilot will conduct a preflight inspection of the aircraft. If any irregularities' are found in the inspection, they must be corrected before the small UA is operated. Some small UA manufacturers will provide the remote pilot with preflight inspection items. For those small UAs that do not have a manufacturer checklist, the remote should develop a checklist that will provide enough information that the aircraft will be operated in a safe condition.

When a remote pilot does experience an inflight emergency, the pilot may take any action to ensure that there is not a hazard to other people or property. For example, if during a flight the small UA experiences as battery fire, the remote pilot may need to climb the small UA above 400' AGL to maneuver to a safe landing area. In this instance, a report will need to be made only if asked to do so by the FAA.

When other crew members are used during a flight, all of those crew members must be briefed on the flight and the planned emergency procedures for the flight. The briefing will be given to any visual observers (VO) that might be used and any non-certificated person who is allowed to manipulate the flight controls of the small UA.

For more information about emergencies, refer to 14 CFR part 107 and AC 107-2.

This page intentionally left blank.

Chapter 6:
Crew Resource Management

For information on Crew Resource Management (CRM), refer to <u>Chapter 10</u>, "Aeronautical Decision-Making and Judgment," of this study guide.

This page intentionally left blank.

Remote Pilot – Small Unmanned Aircraft Systems Study Guide

Chapter 7:
Radio Communication Procedures

Introduction

Radio communications are an important aspect for the safe operation of aircraft in the NAS. It is through radio communications that pilots give and receive information before, during and at the conclusion of a flight. This information aids in the flow of aircraft in highly complex airspace areas as well as in less populated areas. Pilots can also send and receive important safety of flight issues such as unexpected weather conditions, and inflight emergencies. Although small UA pilots are not expected to communicate over radio frequencies, it is important for the UA pilot to understand "aviation language" and the different conversations they will encounter if the UA pilot is using a radio to aid them in situational awareness when operating in the NAS. Although much of the information provided here is geared toward manned aircraft pilots, the UA pilot needs to understand the unique way information is exchanged in the NAS.

Understanding Proper Radio Procedures

Understanding proper radio phraseology and procedures contribute to a pilot's ability to operate safely and efficiently in the airspace system. A review of the Pilot/Controller Glossary contained in the AIM assists a pilot in understanding standard radio terminology. The AIM also contains many examples of radio communications.

ICAO has adopted a phonetic alphabet that should be used in radio communications. When communicating with ATC, pilots should use this alphabet to identify their aircraft. [Figure 7-1]

Traffic Advisory Practices at Airports without Operating Control Towers

Airport Operations without Operating Control Tower

There is no substitute for alertness while in the vicinity of an airport. It is essential that pilots be alert and look for other traffic a when operating at an airport without an operating control tower. This is of particular importance since other aircraft may not have communication capability or, in some cases, pilots may not communicate their presence or intentions when operating into or out of such airports. To achieve the greatest degree of safety, it is essential that all radio-equipped aircraft transmit/receive on a common frequency and small UA pilots monitor other aircraft identified for the purpose of airport advisories.

An airport may have a full or part-time tower or flight

Character	Morse Code	Telephony	Phonic Pronunciation
A	•—	Alfa	(AL-FAH)
B	—•••	Bravo	(BRAH-VOH)
C	—•—•	Charlie	(CHAR-LEE) or (SHAR-LEE)
D	—••	Delta	(DELL-TAH)
E	•	Echo	(ECK-OH)
F	••—•	Foxtrot	(FOKS-TROT)
G	——•	Golf	(GOLF)
H	••••	Hotel	(HOH-TEL)
I	••	India	(IN-DEE-AH)
J	•———	Juliett	(JEW-LEE-ETT)
K	—•—	Kilo	(KEY-LOH)
L	•—••	Lima	(LEE-MAH)
M	——	Mike	(MIKE)
N	—•	November	(NO-VEM-BER)
O	———	Oscar	(OSS-CAH)
P	•——•	Papa	(PAH-PAH)
Q	——•—	Quebec	(KEH-BECK)
R	•—•	Romeo	(ROW-ME-OH)
S	•••	Sierra	(SEE-AIR-RAH)
T	—	Tango	(TANG-GO)
U	••—	Uniform	(YOU-NEE-FORM) or (OO-NEE-FORM)
V	•••—	Victor	(VIK-TAH)
W	•——	Whiskey	(WISS-KEY)
X	—••—	Xray	(ECKS-RAY)
Y	—•——	Yankee	(YANG-KEY)
Z	——••	Zulu	(ZOO-LOO)
1	•————	One	(WUN)
2	••———	Two	(TOO)
3	•••——	Three	(TREE)
4	••••—	Four	(FOW-ER)
5	•••••	Five	(FIFE)
6	—••••	Six	(SIX)
7	——•••	Seven	(SEV-EN)
8	———••	Eight	(AIT)
9	————•	Nine	(NIN-ER)
0	—————	Zero	(ZEE-RO)

Figure 7-1. *Phonetic Alphabet.*

service station (FSS) located on the airport, a full or part-time universal communications (UNICOM) station or no aeronautical station at all. There are three ways for pilots to communicate their intention and obtain airport/traffic information when operating at an airport that does not have an operating tower—by communicating with an FSS, a UNICOM operator, or by making a self-announce broadcast.

Many airports are now providing completely automated weather, radio check capability and airport advisory information on an automated UNICOM system. These systems offer a variety of features, typically selectable by microphone clicks, on the UNICOM frequency. Availability of the automated UNICOM will be published in the Airport/Facility Directory and approach charts.

Understanding Communication on a Common Frequency

The key to communications at an airport without an operating control tower is selection of the correct common frequency. The acronym CTAF, which stands for Common Traffic Advisory Frequency, is synonymous with this program. A CTAF is a frequency designated for the purpose of carrying out airport advisory practices while operating to or from an airport without an operating control tower. The CTAF may be a UNICOM, MULTICOM, FSS, or tower frequency and is identified in appropriate aeronautical publications.

Communication/Broadcast Procedures

A MULTICOM frequency of 122.9 will be used at an airport that is non-towered and does not have a FSS or UNICOM.

Recommended Traffic Advisory Practices

Although a remote pilot-in-command is not required to communicate with manned aircraft when in the vicinity of a non-towered airport, safety in the National Airspace System requires that remote pilots are familiar with traffic patterns, radio procedures, and radio phraseology.

When a remote pilot plans to operate close to a non-towered airport, the first step in radio procedures is to identify the appropriate frequencies. Most non-towered airports will have a UNICOM frequency, which is usually 122.8; however, you should always check the Cart Supplements U.S. or sectional chart for the correct frequency. This frequency can vary when there are a large number of non-towered airports in the area. For non-towered airports that do not have a UNICOM or any other frequency listed, the MULTICOM frequency of 122.9 will be used. These frequencies can be found on a sectional chart by the airport or in the Chart Supplements publication from the FAA.

When a manned aircraft is inbound to a non-towered airport, the standard operating practice is for the pilot to "broadcast in the blind" when 10 miles from the airport. This initial radio call will also include the position the aircraft is in relation to north, south, east or west from the airport. For example:

> *Town and Country traffic, Cessna 123 Bravo Foxtrot is 10 miles south inbound for landing, Town and Country traffic.*

When a manned aircraft is broadcasting at a non-towed airport, the aircraft should use the name of the airport of intended landing at the beginning of the broadcast, and again at the end of the broadcast. The reason for stating the name twice is to allow others who are on the frequency to confirm where the aircraft is going. The next broadcast that the manned aircraft should make is:

> *Town and Country traffic, Cessna 123 Bravo Foxtrot, is entering the pattern, mid-field left down-wind for runway 18, Town and Country traffic.*

The aircraft is now entering the traffic pattern. In this example, the aircraft is making a standard 45 degree entry to the downwind leg of the pattern for runway 18. Or, the aircraft could land straight-in without entering the typical rectangular traffic pattern. Usually aircraft that are executing an instrument approach will use this method. Examples of a radio broadcast from aircraft that are using this technique are:

For an aircraft that is executing an instrument approach:

> *Town and Country traffic, Cessna 123 Bravo Foxtrot, is one mile north of the airport, GPS runway 18, full stop landing, Town and Country traffic.*

As the aircraft flies the traffic pattern for a landing, the following radio broadcasts should be made:

> *Town and Country traffic, Cessna 123 Bravo Foxtrot, left base, runway 18, Town and Country traffic.*

> *Town and Country traffic, Cessna 123 Bravo Foxtrot, final, runway 18, Town and Country traffic.*

After the aircraft has landed and is clear of the runway, the following broadcast should be made:

> *Town and Country traffic, Cessna 123 Bravo Foxtrot, is clear of runway 18, taxing to park, Town and Country traffic.*

When an aircraft is departing a non-towered airport, the same procedures apply. For example, when the aircraft is ready for takeoff, the aircraft should make the following broadcast:

> *Town and Country traffic, Cessna 123 Bravo Foxtrot, departing runway 18, Town and Country traffic.*

For safety reasons, a remote pilot must always scan the area where they are operating a small UA. This is especially important around an airport. While it is good operating procedures for manned aircraft to make radio broadcasts in the vicinity of a non-towered airport, by regulation, it is not mandatory. For this reason, a remote pilot must always look for other aircraft in the area, and use a radio for an extra layer of situational awareness.

Aircraft Call Signs

When operating in the vicinity of any airport, either towered or non-towered, it is important for a remote pilot to understand radio communications of manned aircraft in the area. Although 14 CFR part 107 only requires the remote pilot to receive authorization to operate in certain airport areas, it can be a good operating practice to have a radio that will allow the remote pilot to monitor the appropriate frequencies in the area. The remote pilot should refrain from transmitting over any active aviation frequency unless there is an emergency situation.

Aviation has unique communication procedures that will be foreign to a remote pilot who has not been exposed to "aviation language" previously. One of those is aircraft call signs. All aircraft that are registered in the United States will have a unique registration number, or "N" number. For example, N123AB, which would be pronounced in aviation terms by use of the phonetic alphabet as, "November One-Two-Three-Alpha-Bravo." In most cases, "November" will be replaced with either the aircraft manufacturer's name (make) and in some cases, the type of aircraft (model). Usually, when the aircraft is a light general aviation (GA) aircraft, the manufacturer's name will be used. In this case, if N123AB is a Cessna 172, the call sign would be "Cessna, One-Two-Three-Alpha-Bravo." If the aircraft is a heavier GA aircraft, such as a turbo-prop, or turbo-jet, the aircraft's model will be used in the call sign. If N123AB is a Cessna Citation, the call sign would be stated as, "Citation, One-Two-Three-Alpha-Bravo." Typically, airliners will use the name of their companies and their flight number in their call signs. For example, Southwest Airlines flight 711, would be said as, "Southwest-Seven-One-One." There are a few airlines such as British Airways who will not use the company name in their call sign. For example, British Airways uses "Speedbird."

To close, a remote pilot is not expected to communicate with other aircraft in the vicinity of an airport, and should not do so unless there is an emergency situation. However, in the interest of safety in the NAS, it is important that a remote pilot understands the aviation language and the types of aircraft that can be operating in the same area as a small UA.

Chapter 8:
Determining the Performance of Small Unmanned Aircraft

Introduction

The manufacturer may provide operational and performance information that contains the operational performance data for the aircraft such as data pertaining to takeoff, climb, range, endurance, descent, and landing. To be able to make practical use of the aircraft's capabilities and limitations, it is essential to understand the significance of the operational data. The use of this data in flying operations is essential for safe and efficient operation. It should be emphasized that the manufacturers' information regarding performance data is not standardized. If manufacturer-published performance data is unavailable, it is advisable to seek out performance data that may have already been determined and published by other users of the same small UA manufacturer model and use that data as a starting point.

Effect of Temperature on Density

Increasing the temperature of a substance decreases its density. Conversely, decreasing the temperature increases the density. Thus, the density of air varies inversely with temperature. This statement is true only at a constant pressure.

In the atmosphere, both temperature and pressure decrease with altitude and have conflicting effects upon density. However, a fairly rapid drop in pressure as altitude increases usually has a dominating effect. Hence, pilots can expect the density to decrease with altitude.

Effect of Humidity (Moisture) on Density

The preceding paragraphs refer to air that is perfectly dry. In reality, it is never completely dry. The small amount of water vapor suspended in the atmosphere may be almost negligible under certain conditions, but in other conditions humidity may become an important factor in the performance of an aircraft. Water vapor is lighter than air; consequently, moist air is lighter than dry air. Therefore, as the water content of the air increases, the air becomes less dense, increasing density altitude and decreasing performance. It is lightest or least dense when, in a given set of conditions, it contains the maximum amount of water vapor.

Humidity, also called relative humidity, refers to the amount of water vapor contained in the atmosphere and is expressed as a percentage of the maximum amount of water vapor the air can hold. This amount varies with temperature. Warm air holds more water vapor, while cold air holds less. Perfectly dry air that contains no water vapor has a relative humidity of zero percent, while saturated air, which cannot hold any more water vapor, has a relative humidity of 100 percent. Humidity alone is usually not considered an important factor in calculating density altitude and aircraft performance, but it is a contributing factor.

This page intentionally left blank.

Chapter 9:
Physiological Factors (Including Drugs and Alcohol) Affecting Pilot Performance

Introduction

14 CFR part 107 does not allow operation of small UA if the remote PIC, the person manipulating the controls, or Visual Observer (VO) is unable to safely carry out his or her responsibilities. It is the remote PIC's responsibility to ensure all crewmembers are not participating in the operation while impaired. While drug and alcohol use are known to impair judgment, certain over-the-counter (OTC) medications and medical conditions could also affect the ability to safely operate a small UA. For example, certain antihistamines and decongestants may cause drowsiness. We also emphasize that part 107 prohibits a person from serving as a remote PIC, person manipulating the controls, VO, or other crewmember if he or she:

- Has consumed any alcoholic beverage within the preceding 8 hours
- Is under the influence of alcohol
- Has a blood alcohol concentration of .04 percent or greater
- Is using a drug that affects the person's mental or physical capabilities.

There are certain medical conditions, such as epilepsy, may also create a risk to operations. It is the remote PIC's responsibility to determine that their medical condition is under control and they can safely conduct a small UA operation.

Physiological/Medical Factors that Affect Pilot Performance

Important medical factors that a pilot should be aware of include the following:

- hyperventilation
- stress
- fatigue
- dehydration
- heatstroke
- the effects of alcohol and drugs

Hyperventilation

Hyperventilation is the excessive rate and depth of respiration leading to abnormal loss of carbon dioxide from the blood. This condition occurs more often among pilots than is generally recognized. It seldom incapacitates completely, but it causes disturbing symptoms that can alarm the uninformed pilot. In such cases, increased breathing rate and anxiety further aggravate the problem. Hyperventilation can lead to unconsciousness due to the respiratory system's overriding mechanism to regain control of breathing. Pilots encountering an unexpected stressful situation may subconsciously increase their breathing rate.

Common symptoms of hyperventilation include:

- Visual impairment
- Unconsciousness
- Lightheaded or dizzy sensation
- Tingling sensations

- Hot and cold sensations
- Muscle spasms

The treatment for hyperventilation involves restoring the proper carbon dioxide level in the body. Breathing normally is both the best prevention and the best cure for hyperventilation. In addition to slowing the breathing rate, breathing into a paper bag or talking aloud helps to overcome hyperventilation. Recovery is usually rapid once the breathing rate is returned to normal.

Stress

Stress is the body's response to physical and psychological demands placed upon it. The body's reaction to stress includes releasing chemical hormones (such as adrenaline) into the blood and increasing metabolism to provide more energy to the muscles. Blood sugar, heart rate, respiration, blood pressure, and perspiration all increase. The term "stressor" is used to describe an element that causes an individual to experience stress. Examples of stressors include physical stress (noise or vibration), physiological stress (fatigue), and psychological stress (difficult work or personal situations).

Stress falls into two broad categories: acute (short term) and chronic (long term). Acute stress involves an immediate threat that is perceived as danger. This is the type of stress that triggers a "fight or flight" response in an individual, whether the threat is real or imagined. Normally, a healthy person can cope with acute stress and prevent stress overload. However, ongoing acute stress can develop into chronic stress.

Chronic stress can be defined as a level of stress that presents an intolerable burden, exceeds the ability of an individual to cope, and causes individual performance to fall sharply. Unrelenting psychological pressures, such as loneliness, financial worries, and relationship or work problems can produce a cumulative level of stress that exceeds a person's ability to cope with the situation. When stress reaches these levels, performance falls off rapidly. Pilots experiencing this level of stress are not safe and should not exercise their airman privileges. Pilots who suspect they are suffering from chronic stress should consult a physician.

Fatigue

Fatigue is frequently associated with pilot error. Some of the effects of fatigue include degradation of attention and concentration, impaired coordination, and decreased ability to communicate. These factors seriously influence the ability to make effective decisions. Physical fatigue results from sleep loss, exercise, or physical work. Factors such as stress and prolonged performance of cognitive work result in mental fatigue.

Like stress, fatigue falls into two broad categories: acute and chronic. Acute fatigue is short term and is a normal occurrence in everyday living. It is the kind of tiredness people feel after a period of strenuous effort, excitement, or lack of sleep. Rest after exertion and 8 hours of sound sleep ordinarily cures this condition.

A special type of acute fatigue is skill fatigue. This type of fatigue has two main effects on performance:

- Timing disruption—appearing to perform a task as usual, but the timing of each component is slightly off. This makes the pattern of the operation less smooth because the pilot performs each component as though it were separate, instead of part of an integrated activity.

- Disruption of the perceptual field—concentrating attention upon movements or objects in the center of vision and neglecting those in the periphery. This is accompanied by loss of accuracy and smoothness in control movements.

Acute fatigue has many causes, but the following are among the most important for the pilot:
- Mild hypoxia (oxygen deficiency)
- Physical stress
- Psychological stress
- Depletion of physical energy resulting from psychological stress
- Sustained psychological stress

Acute fatigue can be prevented by proper diet and adequate rest and sleep. A well-balanced diet prevents the body from needing to consume its own tissues as an energy source. Adequate rest maintains the body's store of vital energy.

Chronic fatigue, extending over a long period of time, usually has psychological roots, although an underlying disease is sometimes responsible. Continuous high-stress levels produce chronic fatigue. Chronic fatigue is not relieved by proper diet and adequate rest and sleep and usually requires treatment by a physician. An individual may experience this condition in the form of weakness, tiredness, palpitations of the heart, breathlessness, headaches, or irritability. Sometimes chronic fatigue even creates stomach or intestinal problems and generalized aches and pains throughout the body. When the condition becomes serious enough, it leads to emotional illness.

If suffering from acute fatigue, a remote pilot should not operate a small UA. If fatigue occurs during the operation of a small UA, no amount of training or experience can overcome the detrimental effects. Getting adequate rest is the only way to prevent fatigue from occurring. Avoid flying a small UA without a full night's rest, after working excessive hours, or after an especially exhausting or stressful day. Remote pilots who suspect they are suffering from chronic fatigue should consult a physician.

Dehydration
Dehydration is the term given to a critical loss of water from the body. Causes of dehydration are hot temperatures, wind, humidity, and diuretic drinks—coffee, tea, alcohol, and caffeinated soft drinks. Some common signs of dehydration are headache, fatigue, cramps, sleepiness, and dizziness.

The first noticeable effect of dehydration is fatigue, which in turn makes top physical and mental performance difficult, if not impossible. Flying a small UA for long periods in hot summer temperatures or at high altitudes increases the susceptibility to dehydration because these conditions tend to increase the rate of water loss from the body.

To help prevent dehydration, drink two to four quarts of water every 24 hours. Since each person is physiologically different, this is only a guide. Most people are aware of the eight-glasses-a-day guide: If each glass of water is eight ounces, this equates to 64 ounces, which is two quarts. If this fluid is not replaced, fatigue progresses to dizziness, weakness, nausea, tingling of hands and feet, abdominal cramps, and extreme thirst.

The key for pilots is to be continually aware of their condition. Most people become thirsty with a 1.5 quart deficit or a loss of 2 percent of total body weight. This level of dehydration triggers the "thirst mechanism." The problem is that the thirst mechanism arrives too late and is turned off too easily. A small amount of fluid in the mouth turns this mechanism off and the replacement of needed body fluid is delayed.

Other steps to prevent dehydration include:

- Carrying a container in order to measure daily water intake.
- Staying ahead—not relying on the thirst sensation as an alarm. If plain water is not preferred, add some sport drink flavoring to make it more acceptable.
- Limiting daily intake of caffeine and alcohol (both are diuretics and stimulate increased production of urine).

Heatstroke

Heatstroke is a condition caused by any inability of the body to control its temperature. Onset of this condition may be recognized by the symptoms of dehydration, but also has been known to be recognized only upon complete collapse.

To prevent these symptoms, it is recommended that an ample supply of water be carried and used at frequent intervals, whether thirsty or not. The body normally absorbs water at a rate of 1.2 to 1.5 quarts per hour. Individuals should drink one quart per hour for severe heat stress conditions or one pint per hour for moderate stress conditions. For more information on water consumption, refer to the "Dehydration" section of this chapter.

Drugs

The Federal Aviation Regulations include no specific references to medication usage. Title 14 of the CFR prohibits acting as PIC or in any other capacity as a required pilot flight crewmember, while that person:

1. Knows or has reason to know of any medical condition that would make the person unable to meet the requirement for the medical certificate necessary for the pilot operation, or
2. Is taking medication or receiving other treatment for a medical condition that results in the person being unable to meet the requirements for the medical certificate necessary for the pilot operation.

Further, 14 CFR part 107 and 14 CFR part 91, sections 91.17 and 91.19 prohibit the use of any drug that affects the person's faculties in any way contrary to safety.

There are several thousand medications currently approved by the U.S. Food and Drug Administration (FDA), not including OTC drugs. Virtually all medications have the potential for adverse side effects in some people. Additionally, herbal and dietary supplements, sport and energy boosters, and some other "natural" products are derived from substances often found in medications that could also have adverse side effects. While some individuals experience no side effects with a particular drug or product, others may be noticeably affected. The FAA regularly reviews FDA and other data to assure that medications found acceptable for aviation duties do not pose an adverse safety risk.

Some of the most commonly used OTC drugs, antihistamines and decongestants, have the potential to cause noticeable adverse side effects, including drowsiness and cognitive deficits. The symptoms associated with common upper respiratory infections, including the common cold, often suppress a pilot's desire to fly, and treating symptoms with a drug that causes adverse side effects only compounds the problem. Particularly, medications containing diphenhydramine (e.g., Benadryl) are known to cause drowsiness and have a prolonged half-life, meaning the drugs stay in one's system for an extended time, which lengthens the time that side effects are present.

Prior to each and every flight, all pilots must do a proper physical self-assessment to ensure safety. A great mnemonic is IMSAFE, which stands for Illness, Medication, Stress, Alcohol, Fatigue, and Emotion.

For the medication component of IMSAFE, pilots need to ask themselves, "Am I taking any medicines that might affect my judgment or make me drowsy? For any new medication, OTC or prescribed, you should wait at least 48 hours after the first dose before flying to determine you do not have any adverse side effects that would make it unsafe to operate an aircraft. In addition to medication questions, pilots should also consider the following:

- Do not take any unnecessary or elective medications.
- Make sure you eat regular balanced meals.
- Bring a snack.
- Maintain good hydration - bring plenty of water.
- Ensure adequate sleep the night prior to the flight.
- Stay physically fit.

Alcohol

Alcohol impairs the efficiency of the human body. *[Figure 9-1]* Studies have shown that consuming alcohol is closely linked to performance deterioration. Pilots must make hundreds of decisions, some of them time-critical, during the course of a flight. The safe outcome of any flight depends on the ability to make the correct decisions and take the appropriate actions during routine occurrences, as well as abnormal situations. The influence of alcohol drastically reduces the chances of completing a flight without incident. Even in small amounts, alcohol can impair judgment, decrease sense of responsibility, affect coordination, constrict visual field, diminish memory, reduce reasoning ability, and lower attention span. As little as one ounce of alcohol can decrease the speed and strength of muscular reflexes, lessen the efficiency of eye movements while reading, and increase the frequency at which errors are committed. Impairments in vision and hearing can occur from consuming as little as one drink.

While experiencing a hangover, a pilot is still under the influence of alcohol. Although a pilot may think he or she is functioning normally, motor and mental response impairment is still present. Considerable amounts of alcohol can remain in the body for over 16 hours, so pilots should be cautious about flying too soon after drinking.

Type Beverage	Typical Serving (oz)	Pure Alcohol Content (oz)
Table wine	4.0	.48
Light beer	12.0	.48
Aperitif liquor	1.5	.38
Champagne	4.0	.48
Vodka	1.0	.50
Whiskey	1.25	.50

0.01–0.05% (10–50 mg)	average individual appears normal
0.03–0.12%* (30–120 mg)	mild euphoria, talkativeness, decreased inhibitions, decreased attention, impaired judgment, increased reaction time
0.09–0.25% (90–250 mg)	emotional instability, loss of critical judgment, impairment of memory and comprehension, decreased sensory response, mild muscular incoordination
0.18–0.30% (180–300 mg)	confusion, dizziness, exaggerated emotions (anger, fear, grief), impaired visual perception, decreased pain sensation, impaired balance, staggering gait, slurred speech, moderate muscular incoordination
0.27–0.40% (270–400 mg)	apathy, impaired consciousness, stupor, significantly decreased response to stimulation, severe muscular incoordination, inability to stand or walk, vomiting, incontinence of urine and feces
0.35–0.50% (350–500 mg)	unconsciousness, depressed or abolished re exes, abnormal body temperature, coma, possible death from respiratory paralysis (450 mg or above)

* Legal limit for motor vehicle operation in most states is 0.08 or 0.10% (80–100 mg of alcohol per dL of blood).

Figure 9-1. *Impairment scale with alcohol use.*

Intoxication is determined by the amount of alcohol in the bloodstream. This is usually measured as a percentage by weight in the blood. 14 CFR part 91 requires that blood alcohol level be less than .04 percent and that 8 hours pass between drinking alcohol and piloting an aircraft. A pilot with a blood alcohol level of .04 percent or greater after 8 hours cannot fly until the blood alcohol falls below that amount. Even though blood alcohol may be well below .04 percent, a pilot cannot fly sooner than 8 hours after drinking alcohol. Although the regulations are quite specific, it is a good idea to be more conservative than the regulations.

Vision and Flight

The more a pilot understands about the eyes and how they function, the easier it is to use vision effectively and compensate for potential problems.

Scanning Techniques

To scan effectively, pilots must look from right to left or left to right. They should begin scanning at the greatest distance an object can be perceived (top) and move inward toward the position of the aircraft (bottom). For each stop, an area approximately 30° wide should be scanned. The duration of each stop is based on the degree of detail that is required, but no stop should last longer than 2 to 3 seconds. When moving from one viewing point to the next, pilots should overlap the previous field of view by 10°. [Figure 9-2]

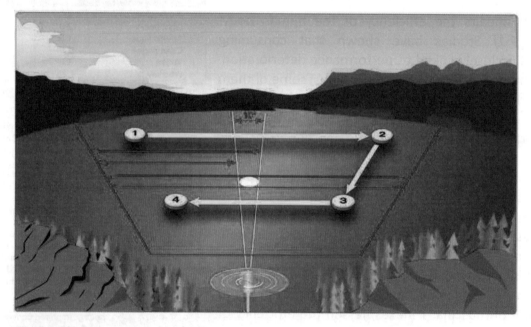

Figure 9-2. *Scanning techniques.*

Chapter 10:
Aeronautical Decision-Making and Judgment

Introduction

Aeronautical decision-making (ADM) is decision-making in a unique environment—aviation. It is a systematic approach to the mental process used by pilots to consistently determine the best course of action in response to a given set of circumstances. It is what a pilot intends to do based on the latest information he or she has.

The importance of learning and understanding effective ADM skills cannot be overemphasized. While progress is continually being made in the advancement of pilot training methods, aircraft equipment and systems, and services for pilots, accidents still occur. Despite all the changes in technology to improve flight safety, one factor remains the same: the human factor which leads to errors. It is estimated that approximately 80 percent of all aviation accidents are related to human factors and the vast majority of these accidents occur during landing (24.1 percent) and takeoff (23.4 percent).

ADM is a systematic approach to risk assessment and stress management. To understand ADM is to also understand how personal attitudes can influence decision-making and how those attitudes can be modified to enhance safety in the operation of a small UA. It is important to understand the factors that cause humans to make decisions and how the decision-making process not only works, but can be improved.

History of ADM

For over 25 years, the importance of good pilot judgment, or aeronautical decision-making (ADM), has been recognized as critical to the safe operation of aircraft, as well as accident avoidance. The airline industry, motivated by the need to reduce accidents caused by human factors, developed the first training programs based on improving ADM. Crew resource management (CRM) training for flight crews is focused on the effective use of all available resources: human resources, hardware, and information supporting ADM to facilitate crew cooperation and improve decision-making. The goal of all flight crews is good ADM and the use of CRM is one way to make good decisions.

Research in this area prompted the Federal Aviation Administration (FAA) to produce training directed at improving the decision-making of pilots and led to current FAA regulations that require that decision-making be taught as part of the pilot training curriculum. Aeronautical Decision Making and Risk Management are topics that the FAA is required to test an applicant about for the issuance of an sUAS certificate. ADM research, development, and testing culminated in 1987 with the publication of six manuals oriented to the decision-making needs of variously rated pilots. These manuals provided multifaceted materials designed to reduce the number of decision-related accidents. The effectiveness of these materials was validated in independent studies where student pilots received such training in conjunction with the standard flying curriculum. When tested, the pilots who had received ADM-training made fewer inflight errors than those who had not received ADM training. The differences were statistically significant and ranged from about 10 to 50 percent fewer judgment errors. In the operational environment, an operator flying about 400,000 hours annually demonstrated a 54 percent reduction in accident rate after using these materials for recurrency training.

Contrary to popular opinion, good judgment can be taught. Tradition held that good judgment was a natural by-product of experience, but as pilots continued to log accident-free flight hours, a corresponding increase of good judgment was assumed. Building upon the foundation of conventional decision-making, ADM enhances the process to decrease the probability of human error and increase the probability of a safe flight. ADM provides a structured, systematic approach to analyzing changes that occur during a flight and how these changes might affect the safe outcome of a flight. The ADM process addresses all aspects of decision-making and identifies the steps involved in good decision-making.

Steps for good decision-making are:

1. Identifying personal attitudes hazardous to safe flight.
2. Learning behavior modification techniques.
3. Learning how to recognize and cope with stress.
4. Developing risk assessment skills.
5. Using all resources.
6. Evaluating the effectiveness of one's ADM skills.

Risk Management

The goal of risk management is to proactively identify safety-related hazards and mitigate the associated risks. Risk management is an important component of ADM. When a pilot follows good decision-making practices, the inherent risk in a flight is reduced or even eliminated. The ability to make good decisions is based upon direct or indirect experience and education. The formal risk management decision-making process involves six steps as shown in *Figure 10-1*.

Figure 10-1. *Risk management decision-making process.*

Consider automotive seat belt use. In just two decades, seat belt use has become the norm, placing those who do not wear seat belts outside the norm, but this group may learn to wear a seat belt by either direct or indirect experience. For example, a driver learns through direct experience about the value of wearing a seat belt when he or she is involved in a car accident that leads to a personal injury. An indirect learning experience occurs when a loved one is injured during a car accident because he or she failed to wear a seat belt.

As you work through the ADM cycle, it is important to remember the four fundamental principles of risk management.

1. Accept no unnecessary risk. Flying is not possible without risk, but unnecessary risk comes without a corresponding return.
2. Make risk decisions at the appropriate level. Risk decisions should be made by the person who can develop and implement risk controls.
3. Accept risk when benefits outweigh dangers (costs).

4. Integrate risk management into planning at all levels. Because risk is an unavoidable part of every flight, safety requires the use of appropriate and effective risk management not just in the preflight planning stage, but in all stages of the flight.

While poor decision-making in everyday life does not always lead to tragedy, the margin for error in aviation is thin. Since ADM enhances management of an aeronautical environment, all pilots should become familiar with and employ ADM.

Crew Resource Management (CRM) and Single-Pilot Resource Management

While CRM focuses on pilots operating in crew environments, many of the concepts apply to single-pilot operations. Many CRM principles have been successfully applied to single-pilot aircraft and led to the development of Single-Pilot Resource Management (SRM). SRM is defined as the art and science of managing all the resources available to a single pilot (prior to and during flight) to ensure the successful outcome of the flight. SRM includes the concepts of ADM, risk management (RM), task management (TM), automation management (AM), controlled flight into terrain (CFIT) awareness, and situational awareness (SA). SRM training helps the pilot maintain situational awareness by managing the automation and associated aircraft control and navigation tasks. This enables the pilot to accurately assess and manage risk and make accurate and timely decisions.

SRM is all about helping pilots learn how to gather information, analyze it, and make decisions.

Hazard and Risk

Two defining elements of ADM are hazard and risk. Hazard is a real or perceived condition, event, or circumstance that a pilot encounters. When faced with a hazard, the pilot makes an assessment of that hazard based upon various factors. The pilot assigns a value to the potential impact of the hazard, which qualifies the pilot's assessment of the hazard—risk.

Therefore, risk is an assessment of the single or cumulative hazard facing a pilot; however, different pilots see hazards differently.

Hazardous Attitudes and Antidotes

Being fit to fly depends on more than just a pilot's physical condition and recent experience. For example, attitude affects the quality of decisions. Attitude is a motivational predisposition to respond to people, situations, or events in a given manner. Studies have identified five hazardous attitudes that can interfere with the ability to make sound decisions and exercise authority properly: anti-authority, impulsivity, invulnerability, macho, and resignation. *[Figure 10-2]*

Hazardous attitudes contribute to poor pilot judgment but can be effectively counteracted by redirecting the hazardous attitude so that correct action can be taken. Recognition of hazardous thoughts is the first step toward neutralizing them. After recognizing a thought as hazardous, the pilot should label it as hazardous, then state the corresponding antidote. Antidotes should be memorized for each of the hazardous attitudes so they automatically come to mind when needed.

The Five Hazardous Attitudes	Antidote
Anti-authority: "Don't tell me." This attitude is found in people who do not like anyone telling them what to do. In a sense, they are saying, "No one can tell me what to do." They may be resentful of having someone tell them what to do or may regard rules, regulations, and procedures as silly or unnecessary. However, it is always your prerogative to question authority if you feel it is in error.	Follow the rules. They are usually right.
Impulsivity: "Do it quickly." This is the attitude of people who frequently feel the need to do something, anything, immediately. They do not stop to think about what they are about to do, they do not select the best alternative, and they do the first thing that comes to mind.	Not so fast. Think first.
Invulnerability: "It won't happen to me." Many people falsely believe that accidents happen to others, but never to them. They know accidents can happen, and they know that anyone can be affected. However, they never really feel or believe that they will be personally involved. Pilots who think this way are more likely to take chances and increase risk.	It could happen to me.
Macho: "I can do it." Pilots who are always trying to prove that they are better than anyone else think, "I can do it—I'll show them." Pilots with this type of attitude will try to prove themselves by taking risks in order to impress others. While this pattern is thought to be a male characteristic, women are equally susceptible.	Taking chances is foolish.
Resignation: "What's the use?" Pilots who think, "What's the use?" do not see themselves as being able to make a great deal of difference in what happens to them. When things go well, the pilot is apt to think that it is good luck. When things go badly, the pilot may feel that someone is out to get them or attribute it to bad luck. The pilot will leave the action to others, for better or worse. Sometimes, such pilots will even go along with unreasonable requests just to be a "nice guy."	I'm not helpless. I can make a difference.

Figure 10-2. *The five hazardous attitudes identified through past and contemporary study.*

Risk

During each flight, the single pilot makes many decisions under hazardous conditions. To fly safely, the pilot needs to assess the degree of risk and determine the best course of action to mitigate the risk.

Assessing Risk

For the single pilot, assessing risk is not as simple as it sounds. For example, the pilot acts as his or her own quality control in making decisions. If a fatigued pilot who has flown 16 hours is asked if he or she is too tired to continue flying, the answer may be "no." Most pilots are goal oriented and when asked to accept a flight, there is a tendency to deny personal limitations while adding weight to issues not germane to the mission. For example, pilots of helicopter emergency services (EMS) have been known (more than other groups) to make flight decisions that add significant weight to the patient's welfare. These pilots add weight to intangible factors (the patient in this case) and fail to appropriately quantify actual hazards, such as fatigue or weather, when making flight decisions. The single pilot who has no other crew member for consultation must wrestle with the intangible factors that draw one into a hazardous position. Therefore, he or she has a greater vulnerability than a full crew.

Mitigating Risk

Risk assessment is only part of the equation.

One of the best ways single pilots can mitigate risk is to use the IMSAFE checklist to determine physical and mental readiness for flying:

1. Illness—Am I sick? Illness is an obvious pilot risk.
2. Medication—Am I taking any medicines that might affect my judgment or make me drowsy?
3. Stress—Am I under psychological pressure from the job? Do I have money, health, or family problems? Stress causes concentration and performance problems. While the regulations list medical conditions that require grounding, stress is not among them. The pilot should consider the effects of stress on performance.
4. Alcohol—Have I been drinking within 8 hours? Within 24 hours? As little as one ounce of liquor, one bottle of beer, or four ounces of wine can impair flying skills. Alcohol also renders a pilot more susceptible to disorientation and hypoxia.
5. Fatigue—Am I tired and not adequately rested? Fatigue continues to be one of the most insidious hazards to flight safety, as it may not be apparent to a pilot until serious errors are made.
6. Emotion—Am I emotionally upset?

The PAVE Checklist

Another way to mitigate risk is to perceive hazards. By incorporating the PAVE checklist into preflight planning, the pilot divides the risks of flight into four categories: **P**ilot-in-command (PIC), **A**ircraft, en**V**ironment, and **E**xternal pressures (PAVE) which form part of a pilot's decision-making process.

With the PAVE checklist, pilots have a simple way to remember each category to examine for risk prior to each flight.

Once a pilot identifies the risks of a flight, he or she needs to decide whether the risk, or combination of risks, can be managed safely and successfully. If not, make the decision to cancel the flight. If the pilot decides to continue with the flight, he or she should develop strategies to mitigate the risks. One way a pilot can control the risks is to set personal minimums for items in each risk category. These are limits unique to that individual pilot's current level of experience and proficiency.

P = Pilot-in-Command (PIC)

The pilot is one of the risk factors in a flight. The pilot must ask, "Am I ready for this flight?" in terms of experience, recency, currency, physical, and emotional condition. The IMSAFE checklist provides the answers.

A = Aircraft

What limitations will the aircraft impose upon the trip? Ask the following questions:

- Is this the right aircraft for the flight?
- Am I familiar with and current in this aircraft?
- Can this aircraft carry the planned load?

V = EnVironment

Weather

Weather is a major environmental consideration. Earlier it was suggested pilots set their own personal minimums, especially when it comes to weather. As pilots evaluate the weather for a particular flight, they should consider the following:

- What is the current ceiling and visibility?
- Consider the possibility that the weather may be different than forecast.
- Are there any thunderstorms present or forecast?
- If there are clouds, is there any icing, current or forecast? What is the temperature/dew point spread and the current temperature at altitude?

Terrain

Evaluation of terrain is another important component of analyzing the flight environment.

Airspace

Check the airspace and any temporary flight restriction (TFRs).

E = External Pressures

External pressures are influences external to the flight that create a sense of pressure to complete a flight—often at the expense of safety. Factors that can be external pressures include the following:

- The desire to demonstrate pilot qualifications
- The desire to impress someone (Probably the two most dangerous words in aviation are "Watch this!")
- The pilot's general goal-completion orientation
- Emotional pressure associated with acknowledging that skill and experience levels may be lower than a pilot would like them to be. Pride can be a powerful external factor!

Managing External Pressures

Management of external pressure is the single most important key to risk management because it is the one risk factor category that can cause a pilot to ignore all the other risk factors.

The use of personal standard operating procedures (SOPs) is one way to manage external pressures. The goal is to supply a release for the external pressures of a flight.

Human Factors

Why are human conditions, such as fatigue, complacency and stress, so important in aviation? These conditions, along with many others, are called human factors. Human factors directly cause or contribute to many aviation accidents and have been documented as a primary contributor to more than 70 percent of aircraft accidents.

Typically, human factor incidents/accidents are associated with flight operations but recently have also become a major concern in aviation maintenance and air traffic management as well. Over the past several years, the FAA has made the study and research of human factors a top priority by working closely with engineers, pilots, mechanics, and ATC to apply the latest knowledge about human factors in an effort to help operators and maintainers improve safety and efficiency in their daily operations.

Human factors science, or human factors technologies, is a multidisciplinary field incorporating contributions from psychology, engineering, industrial design, statistics, operations research, and anthropometry. It is a term that covers the science of understanding the properties of human capability, the application of this understanding to the design, development and deployment of systems and services, and the art of ensuring successful application of human factor principles into all aspects of aviation to include pilots, ATC, and aviation maintenance. Human factors is often considered synonymous with CRM or maintenance resource management (MRM) but is really much broader in both its knowledge base and scope. Human factors involves gathering research specific to certain situations (i.e., flight, maintenance, stress levels, knowledge) about human abilities, limitations, and other characteristics and applying it to tool design, machines, systems, tasks, jobs, and environments to produce safe, comfortable, and effective human use. The entire aviation community benefits greatly from human factors research and development as it helps better understand how humans can most safely and efficiently perform their jobs and improve the tools and systems in which they interact.

The Decision-Making Process

An understanding of the decision-making process provides the pilot with a foundation for developing ADM and SRM skills. While some situations, such as engine failure, require an immediate pilot response using established procedures, there is usually time during a flight to analyze any changes that occur, gather information, and assess risks before reaching a decision.

Risk management and risk intervention is much more than the simple definitions of the terms might suggest. Risk management and risk intervention are decision-making processes designed to systematically identify hazards, assess the degree of risk, and determine the best course of action. These processes involve the identification of hazards, followed by assessments of the risks, analysis of the controls, making control decisions, using the controls, and monitoring the results.

The steps leading to this decision constitute a decision-making process. Three models of a structured framework for problem-solving and decision-making are the 5P, the 3P using PAVE, CARE and TEAM, and the DECIDE models. They provide assistance in organizing the decision process. All these models have been identified as helpful to the single pilot in organizing critical decisions.

Single-Pilot Resource Management (SRM)

Single-Pilot Resource Management (SRM) is about how to gather information, analyze it, and make decisions. Learning how to identify problems, analyze the information, and make informed and timely decisions is not as straightforward as the training involved in learning specific maneuvers. Learning how to judge a situation and "how to think" in the endless variety of situations encountered while flying out in the "real world" is more difficult.

There is no one right answer in ADM, rather each pilot is expected to analyze each situation in light of experience level, personal minimums, and current physical and mental readiness level, and make his or her own decision.

Perceive, Process, Perform (3P) Model

The Perceive, Process, Perform (3P) model for ADM offers a simple, practical, and systematic approach that can be used during all phases of flight. To use it, the pilot will:
- Perceive the given set of circumstances for a flight
- Process by evaluating their impact on flight safety
- Perform by implementing the best course of action

Use the Perceive, Process, Perform, and Evaluate method as a continuous model for every aeronautical decision that you make. Although human beings will inevitably make mistakes, anything that you can do to recognize and minimize potential threats to your safety will make you a better pilot.

Depending upon the nature of the activity and the time available, risk management processing can take place in any of three timeframes. *[Figure 10-3]* Most flight training activities take place in the "time-critical" timeframe for risk management. The six steps of risk management can be combined into an easy-to-remember 3P model for practical risk management: Perceive, Process, Perform with the PAVE, CARE and TEAM checklists. Pilots can help perceive hazards by using the PAVE checklist of: Pilot, Aircraft, enVironment, and External pressures. They can process hazards by using the CARE checklist of: Consequences, Alternatives, Reality, External factors. Finally, pilots can perform risk management by using the TEAM choice list of: Transfer, Eliminate, Accept, or Mitigate.

	Strategic	Deliberate	Time-Critical
Purpose	Used in a complex operation (e.g., introduction of new equipment); involves research, use of analysis tools, formal testing, or long term tracking of risks.	Uses experience and brainstorming to identify hazards, assess risks, and develop controls for planning operations, review of standard operating or training procedures, etc.	"On the fly" mental or verbal review using the basic risk management process during the execution phase of an activity.

Figure 10-3. *Risk management processing can take place in any of three timeframes.*

PAVE Checklist: Identify Hazards and Personal Minimums

In the first step, the goal is to develop situational awareness by perceiving hazards, which are present events, objects, or circumstances that could contribute to an undesired future event. In this step, the pilot will systematically identify and list hazards associated with all aspects of the flight: **P**ilot, **A**ircraft, en**V**ironment, and **E**xternal pressures, which makes up the PAVE checklist. *[Figure 10-4]* All four elements combine and interact to create a unique situation for any flight. Pay special attention to the pilot-aircraft combination, and consider whether the combined "pilot-aircraft team" is capable of the mission you want to fly. For example, you may be a very experienced and proficient pilot, but your weather flying ability is still limited if you are flying an unfamiliar aircraft. On the other hand, you may have a new technically advanced aircraft that you have flown for a considerable amount of time.

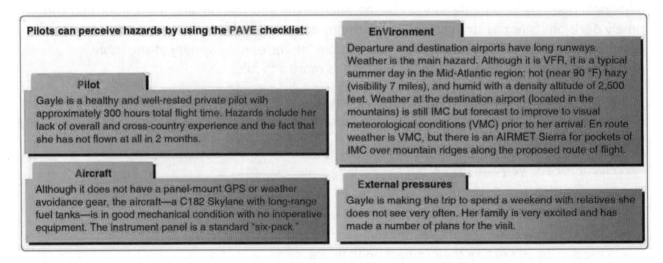

Figure 10-4. *A real-world example of how the 3P model guides decisions on a cross-country trip using the PAVE checklist.*

Decision-Making in a Dynamic Environment

A solid approach to decision-making is through the use of analytical models, such as the 5 Ps, 3P, and DECIDE. Good decisions result when pilots gather all available information, review it, analyze the options, rate the options, select a course of action, and evaluate that course of action for correctness.

In some situations, there is not always time to make decisions based on analytical decision-making skills. A good example is a quarterback whose actions are based upon a highly fluid and changing situation. He intends to execute a plan, but new circumstances dictate decision-making on the fly. This type of decision-making is called automatic decision-making or naturalized decision-making. *[Figure 10-5B]*

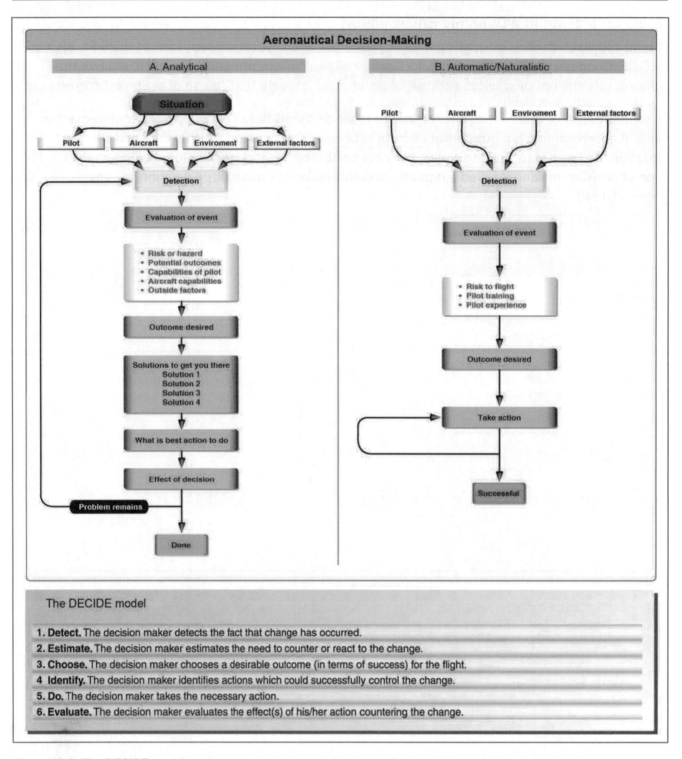

Figure 10-5. *The DECIDE model has been recognized worldwide. Its application is illustrated in column A while automatic/naturalistic decision-making is shown in column B.*

Automatic Decision-Making

For the past several decades, research into how people actually make decisions has revealed that when pressed for time, experts faced with a task loaded with uncertainty first assess whether the situation strikes them as familiar. Rather than comparing the pros and cons of different approaches, they quickly imagine how one or a few possible courses of action in such situations will play out.

Experts take the first workable option they can find. While it may not be the best of all possible choices, it often yields remarkably good results.

The terms "naturalistic" and "automatic decision-making" have been coined to describe this type of decision-making. The ability to make automatic decisions holds true for a range of experts from firefighters to chess players. It appears the expert's ability hinges on the recognition of patterns and consistencies that clarify options in complex situations. Experts appear to make provisional sense of a situation, without actually reaching a decision, by launching experience-based actions that in turn trigger creative revisions.

This is a reflexive type of decision-making anchored in training and experience and is most often used in times of emergencies when there is no time to practice analytical decision-making. Naturalistic or automatic decision-making improves with training and experience, and a pilot will find himself or herself using a combination of decision-making tools that correlate with individual experience and training.

Operational Pitfalls

Although more experienced pilots are likely to make more automatic decisions, there are tendencies or operational pitfalls that come with the development of pilot experience. These are classic behavioral traps into which pilots have been known to fall. More experienced pilots, as a rule, try to complete a flight as planned. The desire to meet these goals can have an adverse effect on safety and contribute to an unrealistic assessment of piloting skills. These dangerous tendencies or behavior patterns, which must be identified and eliminated, include the operational pitfalls shown in *Figure 10-6.*

Operational Pitfalls
Peer pressure
Poor decision-making may be based upon an emotional response to peers, rather than evaluating a situation objectively.
Mindset
A pilot displays mind set through an inability to recognize and cope with changes in a given situation.
Get-there-itis
This disposition impairs pilot judgment through a fixation on the original goal or destination, combined with a disregard for any alternative course of action.
Duck-under syndrome
A pilot may be tempted to make it into an airport by descending below minimums during an approach. There may be a belief that there is a built-in margin of error in every approach procedure, or a pilot may want to admit that the landing cannot be completed and a missed approach must be initiated.
Scud running
This occurs when a pilot tries to maintain visual contact with the terrain at low altitudes while instrument conditions exist.
Continuing visual flight rules (VFR) into Instrument conditions
Spatial disorientation or collision with ground/obstacles may occur when a pilot continues VFR into instrument conditions. This can be even more dangerous if the pilot is not instrument rated or current.
Getting behind the aircraft
This pitfall can be caused by allowing events or the situation to control pilot actions. A constant state of surprise at what happens next may be exhibited when the pilot is getting behind the aircraft.
Loss of positional or situational awareness
In extreme cases, when a pilot gets behind the aircraft, a loss of positional or situational awareness may result. The pilot may not know the aircraft's geographical location or may be unable to recognize deteriorating circumstances.
Operating without adequate fuel reserves
Ignoring minimum fuel reserve requirements is generally the result of overconfidence, lack of flight planning, or disregarding applicable regulations.
Descent below the minimum en route altitude
The duck-under syndrome, as mentioned above, can also occur during the en route portion of an IFR flight.
Flying outside the envelope
The assumed high performance capability of a particular aircraft may cause a mistaken belief that it can meet the demands imposed by a pilot's overestimated flying skills.
Neglect of flight planning, preflight inspections, and checklists
A pilot may rely on short- and long-term memory, regular flying skills, and familiar routes instead of established procedures and published checklists. This can be particularly true of experienced pilots.

Figure 10-6. *Typical operational pitfalls requiring pilot awareness.*

Stress Management

Everyone is stressed to some degree almost all of the time. A certain amount of stress is good since it keeps a person alert and prevents complacency. Effects of stress are cumulative and, if the pilot does not cope with them in an appropriate way, they can eventually add up to an intolerable burden. Performance generally increases with the onset of stress, peaks, and then begins to fall off rapidly as stress levels exceed a person's ability to cope. The ability to make effective decisions during flight can be impaired by stress. There are two categories of stress—acute and chronic. These are both explained in Chapter 9, "Physiological Factors (Including Drugs and Alcohol) Affecting Pilot Performance," of this study guide.

There are several techniques to help manage the accumulation of life stresses and prevent stress overload. For example, to help reduce stress levels, set aside time for relaxation each day or maintain a program of physical fitness. To prevent stress overload, learn to manage time more effectively to avoid pressures imposed by getting behind schedule and not meeting deadlines.

Use of Resources

To make informed decisions during flight operations, a pilot must also become aware of the available resources. Since useful tools and sources of information may not always be readily apparent, learning to recognize these resources is an essential part of ADM training. Resources must not only be identified, but a pilot must also develop the skills to evaluate whether there is time to use a particular resource and the impact its use will have upon the safety of flight.

Stressors
Environmental Conditions associated with the environment, such as temperature and humidity extremes, noise, vibration, and lack of oxygen.
Physiological stress Physical conditions, such as fatigue, lack of physical fitness, sleep loss, missed meals (leading to low blood sugar levels), and illness.
Psychological stress Social or emotional factors, such as a death in the family, a divorce, a sick child, or a demotion at work. This type of stress may also be related to mental workload, such as analyzing a problem, navigating an aircraft, or making decisions.

Figure 10-7. *System stressors. Environmental, physiological, and psychological stress are factors that affect decision-making skills. These stressors have a profound impact especially during periods of high workload.*

Situational Awareness

Situational awareness is the accurate perception and understanding of all the factors and conditions within the five fundamental risk elements (flight, pilot, aircraft, environment, and type of operation that comprise any given aviation situation) that affect safety before, during, and after the flight.

Maintaining situational awareness requires an understanding of the relative significance of all flight related factors and their future impact on the flight. When a pilot understands what is going on and has an overview of the total operation, he or she is not fixated on one perceived significant factor. Not only is it important for a pilot to know the aircraft's geographical location, it is also important he or she understand what is happening.

Obstacles to Maintaining Situational Awareness

Fatigue, stress, and work overload can cause a pilot to fixate on a single perceived important item and reduce an overall situational awareness of the flight. A contributing factor in many accidents is a distraction that diverts the pilot's attention from monitoring the aircraft.

Workload Management

Effective workload management ensures essential operations are accomplished by planning, prioritizing, and sequencing tasks to avoid work overload. As experience is gained, a pilot learns to recognize future workload requirements and can prepare for high workload periods during times of low workload.

In addition, a pilot should listen to ATIS, Automated Surface Observing System (ASOS), or Automated Weather Observing System (AWOS), if available, and then monitor the tower frequency or Common Traffic Advisory Frequency (CTAF) to get a good idea of what traffic conditions to expect.

Recognizing a work overload situation is also an important component of managing workload. The first effect of high workload is that the pilot may be working harder but accomplishing less. As workload increases, attention cannot be devoted to several tasks at one time, and the pilot may begin to focus on one item. When a pilot becomes task saturated, there is no awareness of input from various sources, so decisions may be made on incomplete information and the possibility of error increases.

When a work overload situation exists, a pilot needs to stop, think, slow down, and prioritize. It is important to understand how to decrease workload.

Chapter 11:
Airport Operations

Introduction

The definition for airports refers to any area of land or water used or intended for landing or takeoff of aircraft. This includes, within the five categories of airports listed below, special types of facilities including seaplane bases, heliports, and facilities to accommodate tilt rotor aircraft. An airport includes an area used or intended for airport buildings, facilities, as well as rights of way together with the buildings and facilities.

Types of Airports

There are two types of airports—towered and non-towered. These types can be further subdivided to:

- Civil Airports—airports that are open to the general public.
- Military/Federal Government airports—airports operated by the military, National Aeronautics and Space Administration (NASA), or other agencies of the Federal Government.
- Private Airports—airports designated for private or restricted use only, not open to the general public.

Towered Airport

A towered airport has an operating control tower. Air traffic control (ATC) is responsible for providing the safe, orderly, and expeditious flow of air traffic at airports where the type of operations and/or volume of traffic requires such a service.

Non-towered Airport

A non-towered airport does not have an operating control tower. Two-way radio communications are not required, although it is a good operating practice for pilots to monitor other aircraft on the specified frequency for the benefit of other traffic in the area. The key to monitoring traffic at an airport without an operating control tower is selection of the correct common frequency. The acronym CTAF, which stands for Common Traffic Advisory Frequency, is synonymous with this program. A CTAF is a frequency designated for the purpose of carrying out airport advisory practices while operating to or from an airport without an operating control tower. The CTAF may be a Universal Integrated Community (UNICOM), MULTICOM, FSS, or tower frequency and is identified in appropriate aeronautical publications. UNICOM is a nongovernment air/ground radio communication station that may provide airport information at public use airports where there is no tower or FSS.

Non-towered airport traffic patterns are always entered at pattern altitude. How you enter the pattern depends upon the direction of arrival. The preferred method for entering from the downwind side of the pattern is to approach the pattern on a course 45 degrees to the downwind leg and join the pattern at midfield.

Sources for Airport Data

When a remote pilot operates in the vicinity of an airport, it is important to review the current data for that airport. This data provides the pilot with information, such as communication frequencies, services available, closed runways, or airport construction. Three common sources of information are:

- Aeronautical Charts

- Chart Supplement U.S. (formerly Airport/Facility Directory)
- Notices to Airmen (NOTAMs)
- Automated Terminal Information Service (ATIS)

Chart Supplement U.S. (formerly Airport/Facility Directory)

The Chart Supplement U.S. (formerly Airport/Facility Directory) provides the most comprehensive information on a given airport. It contains information on airports, heliports, and seaplane bases that are open to the public. The Chart Supplement U.S. is published in seven books, which are organized by regions and are revised every 56 days. The Chart Supplement U.S. is also available digitally at www.faa.gov/air_traffic/flight_info/aeronav. *Figure 11-1* contains an excerpt from a directory. For a complete listing of information provided in a Chart Supplement U.S. and how the information may be decoded, refer to the "Legend Sample" located in the front of each Chart Supplement U.S.

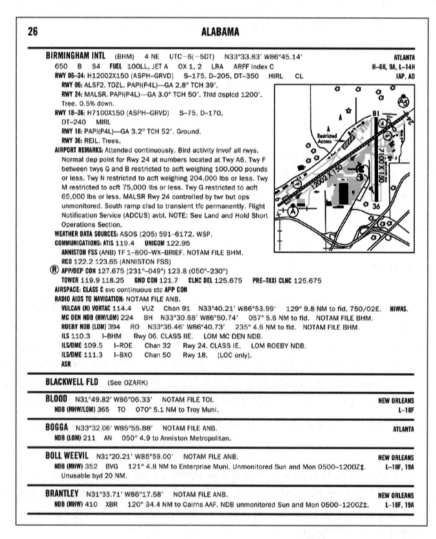

Figure 11-1. *Chart Supplement U.S. (formerly Airport/Facility Directory excerpt.*

Notices to Airmen (NOTAM)

Time-critical aeronautical information, which is of a temporary nature or not sufficiently known in advance to permit publication, on aeronautical charts or in other operational publications, that receives immediate dissemination by the NOTAM system. The NOTAM information could affect your decision to make the flight. Although NOTAMs contain information such as taxiway and runway closures, construction, communications, changes in status of navigational aids, and other information essential to planned en route, terminal, or landing operations, a remote pilot can use this information to help them make an informed decision about where and when to operate their small UA. Exercise good judgment and common sense by carefully regarding the information readily available in NOTAMs.

Prior to any flight, pilots should check for any NOTAMs that could affect their intended flight. For more information on NOTAMs, refer back to Chapter 2, "Airspace Classification, Operating Requirements, and Flight Restrictions," of this study guide.

Automated Terminal Information Service (ATIS)

The Automated Terminal Information Service (ATIS) is a recording of the local weather conditions and other pertinent non-control information broadcast on a local frequency in a looped format. It is normally updated once per hour but is updated more often when changing local conditions warrant. Important information is broadcast on ATIS including weather, runways in use, specific ATC procedures, and any airport construction activity that could affect taxi planning.

When the ATIS is recorded, it is given a code. This code is changed with every ATIS update. For example, ATIS Alpha is replaced by ATIS Bravo. The next hour, ATIS Charlie is recorded, followed by ATIS Delta and progresses down the alphabet.

Aeronautical Charts

An aeronautical chart is the road map for a pilot. The chart provides information that allows remote pilots to obtain information about the areas where they intend to operate. The two aeronautical charts used by VFR pilots are:

- Sectional
- VFR Terminal Area

A free catalog listing aeronautical charts and related publications including prices and instructions for ordering is available at the Aeronautical Navigation Products website: www.aeronav.faa.gov.

Sectional Charts

Sectional charts are the most common charts used by pilots today. The charts have a scale of 1:500,000 (1 inch = 6.86 nautical miles (NM) or approximately 8 statute miles (SM)), which allows for more detailed information to be included on the chart.

The charts provide an abundance of information, including airport data, navigational aids, airspace, and topography. *Figure 11-2* is an excerpt from the legend of a sectional chart. By referring to the chart legend, a pilot can interpret most of the information on the chart. A pilot should also check the chart for other legend information, which includes air traffic control (ATC) frequencies and information on airspace. These charts are revised semiannually except for some areas outside the conterminous United States where they are revised annually.

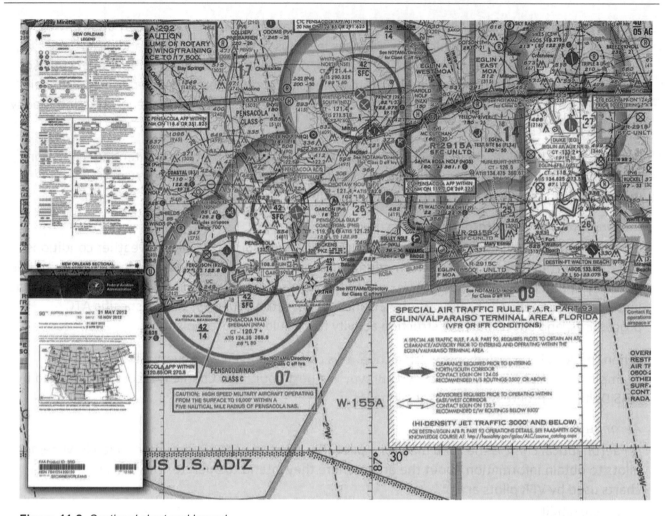

Figure 11-2. *Sectional chart and legend.*

Latitude and Longitude (Meridians and Parallels)

The equator is an imaginary circle equidistant from the poles of the Earth. Circles parallel to the equator (lines running east and west) are parallels of latitude. They are used to measure degrees of latitude north (N) or south (S) of the equator. The angular distance from the equator to the pole is one-fourth of a circle or 90°. The 48 conterminous states of the United States are located between 25° and 49° N latitude. The arrows in *Figure 11-3* labeled "Latitude" point to lines of latitude. Meridians of longitude are drawn from the North Pole to the South Pole and are at right angles to the Equator. The "Prime Meridian," which passes through Greenwich, England, is used as the zero line from which measurements are made in degrees east (E) and west (W) to 180°. The 48 conterminous states of the United States are between 67° and 125° W longitude. The arrows in *Figure 11-3* labeled "Longitude" point to lines

Figure 11-3. *Meridians and parallels—the basis of measuring time, distance, and direction.*

of longitude.

Any specific geographical point can be located by reference to its longitude and latitude. Washington, D.C., for example, is approximately 39° N latitude, 77° W longitude. Chicago is approximately 42° N latitude, 88° W longitude.

Variation

Variation is the angle between true north (TN) and magnetic north (MN). It is expressed as east variation or west variation depending upon whether MN is to the east or west of TN.

The north magnetic pole is located close to 71° N latitude, 96° W longitude and is about 1,300 miles from the geographic or true north pole, as indicated in *Figure 11-4.* If the Earth were uniformly magnetized, the compass needle would point toward the magnetic pole, in which case the variation between TN (as shown by the geographical meridians) and MN (as shown by the magnetic meridians) could be measured at any intersection of the meridians.

Actually, the Earth is not uniformly magnetized. In the United States, the needle usually points in the general direction of the magnetic pole, but it may vary in certain geographical localities by many degrees. Consequently, the exact amount of variation at thousands of selected locations in the United States has been carefully determined. The amount and the direction of variation, which change slightly from time to time, are shown on most aeronautical charts as broken magenta lines called isogonic lines that connect points of equal magnetic variation. (The line connecting points at which there is no variation between TN and MN is the agonic line.) An isogonic chart is shown in *Figure 11-5*. Minor bends and turns in the isogonic and agonic lines are caused by unusual geological conditions affecting magnetic forces in these areas.

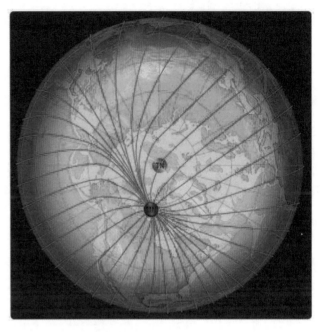

Figure 11-4. *Magnetic meridians are in red while the lines of longitude and latitude are in blue. From these lines of variation (magnetic meridians), on can determine the effect of local magnetic variations on a magnetic compass.*

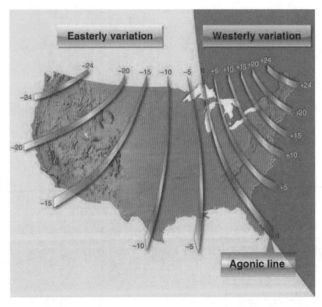

Figure 11-5. *Note the agonic line where magnetic variation is zero.*

Antenna Towers

Extreme caution should be exercised when flying less than 2,000 feet AGL because of numerous skeletal structures, such as radio and television antenna towers, that exceed 1,000 feet AGL with some extending higher than 2,000 feet AGL. Most skeletal structures are supported by guy wires which are very difficult to see in good weather and can be invisible at dusk or during periods of reduced visibility.

These wires can extend about 1,500 feet horizontally from a structure; therefore, all skeletal structures should be avoided horizontally by at least 2,000 feet.

Additionally, new towers may not be on your current chart because the information was not received prior to the printing of the chart.

Chapter 12:
Maintenance and Preflight Inspection Procedures

Maintenance and Preflight Inspection Procedures can be found in chapter 7 of Advisory Circular 107-2.

See the ASA Reader Resource page to review the latest edition of this document: www.asa2fly.com/reader/tpuas

This page intentionally left blank.

Appendix 1:
Study References

Reference	Title
14 CFR part 47	Aircraft Registration
14 CFR part 48	Registration and Marking Requirements for Small Unmanned Aircraft Systems
14 CFR part 71	Designation of Class A, B, C, D and E Airspace Areas; Air Traffic Service Rotes; and Reporting Points
14 CFR part 107	Operation and Certification of Small Unmanned Aircraft Systems
AC 00-6	Aviation Weather for Pilots and Flight Operations Personnel
AC 150/5200-32	Reporting Wildlife Aircraft Strikes
AC 107-2	Small Unmanned Aircraft Systems (sUAS)
AIM	Aeronautical Information Manual
FAA-CT-8080-2	Airman Knowledge Testing Supplement for Sport Pilot, Recreational Pilot, and Private Pilot
FAA-G-8082-20	Remote Pilot Knowledge Test Guide
FAA-H-8083-1	Weight & Balance Handbook
FAA-H-8083-2	Risk Management Handbook
FAA-H-8083-25	Pilot's Handbook of Aeronautical Knowledge
FAA-S-ACS-10	Remote Pilot – Small Unmanned Aircraft Systems Airman Certification Standards
SAFO 09013	Fighting Fires Caused By Lithium Type Batteries in Portable Electronic Devices
SAFO 10015	Flying in the wire environment
SAFO 10017	Risks in Transporting Lithium Batteries in Cargo by Aircraft
SAFO 15010	Carriage of Spare Lithium Batteries in Carry-on and Checked Baggage

Note   *Users should reference the current edition of the reference documents listed above.*

This page intentionally left blank.

Appendix 2:
Registration and Marking Requirements for Small Unmanned Aircraft

Applicants must be familiar with all of the information in 14 CFR part 48, Registration and Marking Requirements for Small Unmanned Aircraft, especially the sections listed in the following table:

Section	Title
48.15	Requirement to register
48.20	Eligibility for registration
48.25	Applicants
48.100	Application
48.205	Display and location of unique identifier

Appendix 3:
Abbreviations and Acronyms

The following abbreviations and acronyms are used in this study guide.

Abb./Acronym	Definition
14 CFR	Title 14 of the Code of Federal Regulations
AC	Advisory Circular
ACS	Airman Certification Standards
ADDS	Aviation Digital Data Services
ADIZ	Air Defense Identification Zone
ADM	Aeronautical Decision-Making
AFM	Airplane Flight Manual
AFS	Flight Standards Service
AGL	Above Ground Level
AIRMET	Airman's Meteorological Information
AOA	Angle of Attack
ATC	Air Traffic Control
ATD	Aviation Training Device
CB	Cumulonimbus
CFA	Controlled Firing Areas
CFR	Code of Federal Regulations
CG	Center of Gravity
CP	Center of Pressure
CRM	Crew Resource Management
CTAF	Common Traffic Advisory Frequency
CTP	Certification Training Program
DPE	Designated Pilot Examiner
DVFR	Defense VFR
EMS	Emergency Services
FAA	Federal Aviation Administration
FADEC	Full Authority Digital Engine Control
FDA	Federal Drug Administration
FDC	Flight Data Center
FL	Flight Level
FRZ	Flight Restriction Zone

Abb./Acronym	Definition
FS	Flight Service
FSDO	Flight Standards District Office
IAP	Instrument Approach Procedures
ICAO	International Civil Aviation Organization
IFR	Instrument Flight Rules
IR	Instrument Routes (sectional charts)
ISA	International Standard Atmosphere
LAA	Local Airport Advisory
MAP	Missed Approach Point
MDA	Minimum Descent Altitude
MEL	Minimum Equipment List
MFD	Multi-functional Displays
MOA	Military Operation Areas
MSL	Mean Sea Level
MTR	Military Training Route
NACG	National Aeronautical Charting Group
NASA	National Aeronautics and Space Administration
NAS	National Airspace System
NM	Nautical Miles
NOAA	National Oceanic and Atmospheric Administration
NOTAM	Notice to Airmen
NSA	National Security Area
OTC	Over-the-Counter
PAVE	PIC – Aircraft – environment – External pressures
POH	Pilot's Operating Handbook
SAO	Special Area of Operation
SIGMET	Significant Meteorological Information
SOP	Standard Operating Procedures
TCU	Towering Cumulus
TFR	Temporary Flight Restrictions
TN	True North
TRSA	Terminal Radar Service Area
TUC	Time of Useful Consciousness
UNICOM	Aeronautical Advisory Communications Stations

Abb./Acronym	Definition
UTC	Coordinated Universal Time
VFR	Visual Flight Rules
VR	Visual Routs (sectional charts)
VO	Visual Observer
W&B	Weight and Balance
WST	Convective Significant Meteorological Information